Edwin Burgis

Perils to British Trade

How to Avert Them

Edwin Burgis

Perils to British Trade
How to Avert Them

ISBN/EAN: 9783744725798

Printed in Europe, USA, Canada, Australia, Japan

Cover: Foto ©ninafisch / pixelio.de

More available books at **www.hansebooks.com**

PERILS TO BRITISH TRADE

HOW TO AVERT THEM

BY

EDWIN BURGIS

LONDON
SWAN SONNENSCHEIN & CO.
NEW YORK: CHARLES SCRIBNER'S SONS
1895

PERILS TO BRITISH

Dedicated

TO

JAMES ANTHONY FROUDE, M.A.

REGIUS PROFESSOR OF HISTORY, OXFORD,

LATE FELLOW OF EXETER COLLEGE, OXFORD,

ETC., ETC.

"The greatness of a nation depends upon the men whom it
can breed and rear."

"The creed of *laissez-faire* is no exposition of eternal principles, but an accident of
the age—a bubble floating upon the river of Time."

NOTE.

PERMISSION for dedication was given by the late Mr. J. A. Froude on May the 18th last, and, on May 23rd, after six chapters were forwarded to Mr. Froude, he wrote :—"So far as I can see I agree heartily with your general views. In detail I can give no opinion without giving more time to the study of them than I can afford. (Mr. Froude was deeply engaged at that time with a series of lectures.) The danger of the present state of things is growing terribly plain to every one who reflects on it. The remedies, I fear, are such as will not be considered till too late to be adopted. As we have sown, we shall have to reap. However, I heartily wish you may succeed in opening blind eyes."

Mr. Froude's fatal illness prevented me from sending Chapter XX.— "Maintain the British Empire by Imperial Commercial Union"—for perusal, which was my earnest desire, in the expectation of receiving a Prefatory Note from England's illustrious writer.

As an enthusiastic admirer of the late historian, and his patriotic principles, and strong appeals to national sentiment, I would say:—

> Great man, thou art gone to thy rest,
> The home of the brave and the free ;
> We mourn, but we think it is best,
> For in death thou shalt stronger be.

E. B.

PREFACE.

POLITICAL authority is now in the hands of the masses of the people, and the system of individualism, established a generation ago, appears to be doomed to destruction.

The political party which formulated its theories has now renounced the creed, and adopted, to a large extent, a socialistic platform.

Yes, the politicians who had no conception of the necessity or utility of the Factory Acts have been succeeded by politicians intent upon legislative interference in every direction, excepting one, namely, the protection of British and Irish labour from the unregulated competition of foreign labour products in British markets.

The recognition by the working classes of Great Britain that a pure individualism is a grinding tyranny, and a deadly struggle of who shall descend first to the lowest level, implies destruction to that wild and unregulated competition in labour (external added to internal) which was introduced by the Free Traders of 1846, and, subsequently, supported as a politico economic system.

The sphere of politics is sure to undergo vast changes when it is rightly understood that the State owes certain duties to its subjects—including the preservation of native industries from ruthless foreign competition.

First of all, the cultivation of the soil, to afford

healthy and natural employment, and to secure for agriculture its *due proportion to other industries.* The utter neglect of British agriculture has had the unhappy effect of congesting labour in the cities and towns.

All who take an intelligent interest in public affairs, and are anxious for the common weal, must be persuaded that the full, varied, and profitable employment of the people is essential to the happiness and power of the State.

How is this consummation to be attained? Only by fiscal regulations instituted by the *collective* action of the community.

The Free Trade reader will, of course, dissent from this statement, as he will probably do with regard to other statements and contentions contained in the following chapters. Now, if the facts, the ideas, and illustrations contained in this work appear somewhat startling, and the Free Trade reader should rush to the conclusion that they must be wrong, the author begs his reader to give these pages a calm and impartial perusal. The subjects examined are full of interest, as they are of importance, to all who wish well for their country and Empire, admitting of no indifference and no postponement.

The advocates of individualism denounced factory and other legislation, as interfering with the " freedom of contract." In their opinion the business of the State was—" to keep the peace, coin money, and leave all the rest to the people." This was the summit of political wisdom.

The reaction from this teaching has at length arrived, and we have loud and general demands for the Government to deal with " *great social problems.*" Here is a new development, and the question of industrial employment must, before long, become the great subject of political discussion.

The swing of the pendulum, from individualism

and a " let alone " policy, to governmental interference
in matters of trade and industry, and involving a
change of colonial policy, is an accomplished fact ;
henceforth we are to witness the interposition of
Government in these matters.

How can the Government interpose to secure fuller
employment for the people except by assuming a
protective and national policy? British industry is
insecure, and the mutual and profitable interchange
of British productions is rendered impossible by our
present fiscal regulations, for instead of varied employment and industrial energy, we observe universal
distrust, confusion and discontent.

It will be strange indeed if the British democracy
hold to the Free Trade formula that " the value of
everything must be settled by universal and unrestricted competition." The British democracy—like
democracies the world over—will rather insist upon
regulating that ceaseless competition which drives
down prices and wages to the lowest possible standard,
and inflicts upon the masses of the population intoler-
able miseries. It will at last perceive that the policy
expressed by that formula is essentially and solely
a capitalistic one, devised and maintained in the
interest alone of the holders and owners of accumulation—the speculative dealers in money and produce,
and those who live upon the interest of exchangeable
investments.

Opportunism is the chief characteristic of present
day politics; clutch at anything and promise anything
to secure popularity. Governments must be "popular,"
and, therefore, socialistic proposals are forthcoming.

But politicians should bear in mind that universal
experience goes to prove that the more popular the
Governments, the more protectionist they become,
particularly when the people have a fixed interest in
production and the cultivation of the soil. Remedial
measures are demanded against " sweating," and the

competition which bears upon the helplessness of the
labourer; the only real remedy for Britain's pressing
need is National Protection, that is, protection to
British and Irish labour; this alone can effectually
develop and maintain the nation's producing forces,
and establish a *true* standard of wages; it is the only
solid foundation for legislating on industrial questions
tending to improve the condition of the working
classes; moreover, it is the only true foundation for
colonisation, and for developing the unparalleled
resources of the British Empire. (See Chapters
XVIII., XIX., and XX.)

When our land is fast going out of cultivation;
when our manufacturing industries are in a condition
of severe depression and decadence; when our population has become congested; when industry does not
co-operate with capital, and both are insecure and
without reward; when we observe in our midst the
striking contrasts of artificial wealth and hopeless
poverty; when we see all these portentous and
gigantic social and industrial evils, present and approaching, surely no apology is needed in raising the
cry of alarm and pointing out, amid the many false
issues, the only true source from whence relief can
come.

The writer gratefully acknowledges the valuable
assistance he has received from his friend, Mr. W. V.
Jackson, of Glasgow, a gentleman who has given
much study to economic and social questions, and
made many sacrifices for the cause of fiscal reform
and Imperial commercial federation of the British
Empire.

E. B

RUSHOLME, MANCHESTER.

CONTENTS.

PERILS TO BRITISH TRADE.

INTRODUCTION.

THE wealth of a country, it has been well said, is " the value of what it produces." Production, therefore, is the basis of national prosperity. In all discussion of questions affecting or related to the material condition of the people—their industries, their earnings, and their savings—this primary and fundamental fact must be borne in mind.

The first indictment, of a popular nature, of Free Trade, and especially of one-sided and partial Free Trade, is, that it imperils and sacrifices national production by the favoured introduction of universal and unreciprocated external competition. There is no possible escape from condemnation on this head for a system which displaces domestic labour by foreign, and reduces to a dangerous and destructive degree the security and remuneration of industrial capital. No one can now deny that this is the result of our present system of *free* import of *competing* foreign productions of land and labour, alongside of the successful maintenance of their protective system

A

by foreign States, and their exhausting revenue
tariffs upon most of what they permit into their
markets of British and Irish production.

It is usual, however, for the professional advocates
of the Free Trade policy of this country to attempt
to justify it, not so much by any defence, or direct
apology for it, on its essential merits, as by inferences
in its favour derived from a misrepresentation of the
policy of Protection. The most systematic and
audacious misrepresentation of facts, and the most
persistent falsification of history, are now the sole
basis for popular belief in it or patience with it.
The Corn Law controversy is falsely described and
disposed of. The temporary and artificial prosperity
of this country during the years of our monopoly of
the improved tools of production and distribution,
and during those years when other great nations
were engaged in exhausting wars—is all ascribed to
the Free Trade policy ; and any attempt or proposal
to revert to fiscal regulation of external trade is
falsely described as limiting the supply of needful
commodities, and attempting to create a monopoly
for landlords. There is, therefore, no scientific defence offered or possible for the present fiscal policy
of Great Britain, but a very unscientific and sense-
less fetish worship is set up in place of critical investigation and fair discussion.

A second popular indictment of our so-called Free
Trade policy is, that it separates and places in
antagonism to each other those elements of the
commonwealth which nature and history have determined to have a common interest. It declares

that the consumer's interest is paramount and opposed to that of the producer; that labour has
separate interests from the capital which employs it,
that one branch of industry in the country has no
interest in the prosperity of any, and of every other,
which is equally possible and natural, and that town
and country have mainly antagonistic interests.
There is here a great field of ethical and philoso-
phical discussion and review of the Individualism of
Free Trade as opposed to the Socialism of Protection,
and several chapters of this book will be devoted to
this most interesting side of the question.

A third indictment of our Free Trade policy is
that it was a rash and precipitate surrender of the
securities for exchange and balance of trade. Its
promoters expected, and predicted, and, no doubt,
devoutly wished, results to happen which they took
no means of ensuring. They placed this country in
the ridiculous position, in a matter of bargain and
balance of interests, of giving an example. The
example of which Great Britain is now the sorry
spectacle, is a solemn warning to every other nation.
It has passed the ridiculous of the confidence trick
victim, and assumed all the tragedy of a *fatal political blunder*. This branch of the subject is capable of
scientific exposition by statistics. The course of trade,
of British external trade, and of British and Irish industrial development, under this policy, compared
with that of foreign industrial nations, is clearly
brought out in the Board of Trade and other official and
statistical returns. The results of that course of trade
are reflected in the social and economic distress, and

the political disturbance with which we are now so painfully familiar.

It is not intended in this book to devote much space to statistics. But a few words now upon the method of understanding statistics of trade will be useful to the reader, who may wish to refer to the official returns, and will make more clear the significance of the tables which will be submitted.

It must be clearly understood that statistics of external trade in themselves afford no evidence of national prosperity. The exhibition of the volume, or the value of total imports and total exports, singly or together, proves nothing apart from, first, the figures relating to domestic production and domestic trade; and, secondly, a discriminating analysis of the nature of the imports and the exports to which the figures refer.

A nation may conceivably be in a very prosperous condition with very little external trade at all. That is, if it has a population equal to the consumption of its own production, and resources equal to all the wants of its increasing population. Its domestic development and domestic exchanges will be the sole, or at least, the chief measure of its prosperity.

Should misfortune and disaster lead to its mortgaging its resources to foreign capitalists, it will then begin to exhibit figures of external trade. It will part with its produce, not for its own comfort and consumption, but in tribute to its foreign conquerors or creditors, and it will have a servile more than a proprietary population. On the other hand, an old, rich, and fully developed country, with no reserve resources, and a population beyond the measure of its production of certain commodities, will exchange in a foreign trade the commodities of which it has a surplus for those commodities in which it is deficient, and figures of external trade will become significant of its prosperity or its decline. But, even here, a balance of trade will require to be maintained, or its capital will be—if its imports continuously exceed its exports [1]—divorced from the interests of its own industries and its own land and labour. Here, also, the imports and exports will require to be classified and analysed before the mere figures can reveal the true nature or value of its external trade.

Such a nation, if it has a sea-board, will be a maritime, and probably also a colonising nation, and its wisdom will be to regard its colonies, however distant, as so many provinces and reserve estates added to its *commonwealth area*, and an artificial extension of its domestic area of production and exchange, which is in its nature more valuable, as Adam Smith clearly shows, than any foreign trade and foreign exchange. Its imports, *if wisdom and statesmanship govern its policy*, will be, raw materials, luxuries which it cannot produce at home, and food products to make up the deficiencies of its domestic supply. Its exports wil be, manufactures beyond the requirements of its own consumption, and it will rigidly conserve all raw materials available for its own use and its own labour, to work up into a currency of employment and exchange.

[1] See Chapter VIII., "The Excess of Imports over Exports and How Paid For."

But all this implies a wise and a scientific protection of its own resources from exploitation by the wild and reckless operation of covetousness and competition by one class or one generation of its population.

If it leaves its trade, and its traders, and its ports, " free " from supervision, encouragement, and restriction suitable to these ends, it will then, first of all, sacrifice its own less fertile and its inland areas ; then it will sacrifice its colonies ; and, lastly, it will sacrifice its manufactures.

Traders trade for profit and not for patriotism. Unless by wise fiscal regulations, it secures that all its own production, home and colonial, shall be economically nearer its markets than those of any foreign State, and unless it has a policy which directs the enterprise of its traders into channels of trade which insure a balance of trade, and, further, insures that it buys from abroad what is to the national interest to buy, and sells in return what it is equally its interest to sell, its volume of trade may be significant only of disaster and national decline.

The Scientific Protection of Foreign Nations illustrates well *their national wisdom*, as does also our one-sided and spurious Free Trade exhibit *our national folly*.

CHAPTER I.

"CONVICTIONS" *re* "FREE TRADE" AND "BARGAINING POWER" CONSIDERED.

The Profession of "Free Trade" Without a Capable and an Independent Judgment—Mr. Cobden's Theory—Great is Diana !—The "Convictions" of Politicians, Professors, and Parsons—The President of the Manchester Statistical Society "born a Free Trader"—The Sycophancy of Free Traders illustrated by Reference to Hamlet and Polonius, Latter-Day Saints, and Bradford "Confessions," Pulpit, Platform, and Press—The Lion on Northumberland House —A Metaphorical Expression—The Wearing Test of Experience—Loss of Bargaining Power.

ARE people convinced about Free Trade? A great many Englishmen *profess* they are convinced as to the wisdom and soundness of our fiscal policy, but we may reasonably conclude that a large proportion of them are not convinced *from capable and independent judgment,* and, therefore, are unable to give valid reasons to support their faith. Moreover, the policy has not yet been submitted to the present extended electorate. There are a number of people who consider that because prosperity followed the adoption of free imports, the system must have caused it. The prosperity came from the making of railways, at home and abroad, the great development of our coal and iron mines, iron manufactures, engineering works, etc., causing an enormous demand for labour; manu-

7

factures came into existence. These various industrial interests acted and re-acted one upon another.

England was *then* "the workshop of the world." Foreign countries purchased railway material and manufactures from us (not producing themselves). All this gave a tremendous impetus to trade, and it was all ascribed to Free Trade, and gave a sort of "mint-mark" to the policy of 1846. English people had unlimited confidence in Mr. Cobden, and indulged the belief that "the commercial salvation of their country was due to this 'prophet.'" Can any sane man at this time entertain any other belief than that Mr. Cobden was utterly mistaken in his prophetic vision? Free Traders, in their heart of hearts, know very well that "the word trade signifies a process of buying and selling, and that without free selling as well as free buying, there can be no real Free Trade." Mr. Cobden did not advocate free buying without *free selling;* "he never advocated the system we are pleased in calling Free Trade, he advocated a theory, conditionally upon the correctness of certain premises. Ample experience proves the premises incorrect, and, consequently, the theory—depending upon them—is invalid." Nations have not come to terms to remit important taxation, so what is the use of holding by fallacies which have, unfortunately, passed muster for common sense? The nostrums of Free Trade are contradicted by the direct evidence of the senses. What about the Free Trader's "convictions"? It is possible that many of them will continue all through to believe in the idol of their worship; they will obstinately cling to the object of their credulity after the fallacy of their faith is demonstrated to unprejudiced minds all around ; they will repair when in difficulty to the feet of their oracle, crying, "Great is Diana !"—their " preserving " goddess, for has not the idol (like the one of old) been represented in the capacity of watching over the poor, and helping the unfortunate ? Tremendous imposture, this goddess of moonshine, for she has not watched over the poor and suffering workers of our country, but whipped them with scorpions, *i.e.*, by imposing upon them an unjust and an artificially stimulated competition.

The gross deception cannot last, as the concentrated labour competition of the whole world attacks English highly-paid labour in its own market, and the situation is becoming unbearable to our workers.

The literature of this generation, particularly schoolroom literature, has supported the system of Free Trade, and the professors of political economy in our colleges have all been in favour of it, giving us their lucubrations on the great science, and the public has listened to the doctrines, and blindly assented without proper investigation. The acceptance of Free Trade has not been a triumph of the intellectual faculty ; the conviction has not come from wise judgment. The spurious conviction has been effected by *mistaking delusion for fact, for the truth of Free Trade has not been revealed by evidence.* Everything that possesses a claim to reasonable belief can be supported by evidence.

The convictions of politicians are referred to in Chapter IX. with becoming reverence. To politicians

we may say, only let British workers (voters) fully
understand that foreigners are doing their work, either
here in the flesh, or by the free importation of cheap
labour products; only let the working classes of
England make it a condition in giving their votes
that British labour must be protected (already there
is a demand for protection from the labour of destitute immigrants), and politicians will at once assume
a different attitude : there will be fresh and extremely
strong convictions of an opposite character. Under
these circumstances what a cut and run there will be !
What a changing of the Free Trade coat for the
Protectionist garment ! Let the popular vote hang
upon this question, and politicians will be converted
wholesale. Some of the readers of this book will
probably live to see this interesting and edifying
spectacle.

There is no reason why an economic question
should be made the shibboleth of party ; but such is
the case. Witness the Cobden Club flap-doodle dispensed in the interests of a political party, to keep
alive the fiction of the " cheap loaf." The delinea-
tion of the idiosyncracies of professing Free Traders
generally is a considerable undertaking. Some years
ago, the writer of this volume had the honour of being
invited by an ancient and learned Manchester society
to hear a paper read upon Free Trade. The president, on introducing the subsequent discussion, remarked that, " so far as he was concerned, there was
nothing to discuss ; he was born a Free Trader ; had
breathed the atmosphere of Free Trade ; he should
live and die a Free Trader whatever might be said to

the contrary." This Free Trader of the "fine old crusted" sort had evidently very strong "convictions;" but he exhibited a peculiar variety of the false art of convincing, which was, in truth, not convincing at all. For this gentleman to have been influenced by arguments and proofs would have only made good the distich of the poet :—

> "He that complies against his will
> Is of his own opinion still."

Doubtless the Free Trade principle is very wonderful, but who would have thought of its being hereditary? The writer has for years examined many processes of reasoning on behalf of Free Trade, but this beats all.

As a rule, the unctuous pronunciation of the phrase, Free Trade (like "that delightful and ever-blessed word Mesopotamia"), has a marvellous effect over weak and subservient minds—a spurious sort of persuasion. This sort of influence is satirised by Shakespeare when he makes the Prince of Denmark cajole the sycophancy of the Lord Chamberlain:—

Hamlet.—Do you see yonder cloud that's almost in shape of a camel?

Polonius.—By the mass, and 'tis like a camel, indeed!

Hamlet.—Methinks it is like a weasel.

Polonius.—It is backed like a weasel.

Hamlet.—Or like a whale?

Polonius.—Very like a whale.

In like manner very goody-goody people have believed all the prophets and latter-day saints of Free Trade have told them :—

Prophets.—Do you see free exchange of untaxed commodities?

Free Traders.—Oh, yes, we see "the beneficent re-sults of free exchange."

Prophets.—Do you see peace and good-will among nations?

Free Traders.—Oh, yes, "we see the ploughshares made of swords, spears, etc., and a commercial mil-lennium approaching."

Latter-Day Saints.—Do you know that if other nations practised Free Trade it would be a bad thing for this country, particularly if America adopted the system?

Free Traders (some years ago).—Oh, yes; "we see the lack of intellect exhibited by foreign nations (to comment on the inaccuracy of Mr. Cobden's pro-phecy would be captious) : they have spurned our offer, they value highly the full and profitable employ-ment of their own labour, but they disregard the in-estimable blessings of buying cheaply." So far as we are concerned, one-sided Free Trade (curious expres-sion) is better than Exchange Trade. We rejoice that other nations are fettered ; it is so much better for us that these fetters should be strengthened. If they were free it would be a bad thing for England.

Free Traders (1894).—Do you know that our hope is in the repeal or modification of the M'Kinley Act?

Free Traders (Bradford, Yorkshire).—Yes; M'Kinley has hit us, and our hopes of the situation being bettered are founded upon a more liberal tariff under Cleveland.

Don't noise it abroad, but it turns out that we have been paying the duties, not the Yankees.

We have learnt by actual experience that it is true that there are fiscal distinctions (the wicked Protectionists have always said so), for we, in Bradford, have paid the duties up to a certain point—prohibition, when we lost the trade. However, we fear the admission, as there are a good many doubting Free Traders in these parts, and we don't like to give ourselves away to the enemy.

Free Traders have been prepared to accept, and in some measure to believe, anything and everything advanced by the prophets and latter-day saints. They have taken their utterances as veritable truths, and fancied themselves convinced, whereas their judgment has been simply overpowered—not by arguments adduced, but by the influence of all the great and good men. Have we not had the beauties of Free Trade extolled from pulpit, platform, and press ? Have not parsons, politicians, and philosophers uttered their benedictions on the great system ? Therefore ordinary mortals, who have not the time or inclination to study the subject for themselves, have responded "Amen" with exceeding docility to the influences named above ; perhaps not in every case has it been a conscious act of submission by the Free Trade disciple—he has simply *fancied himself convinced.*

There is a story of an individual who, by continual looking and hard staring, thought he saw the lion on

Northumberland House wagging its tail, collected a crowd, and worked them into a suitable state of credulity. So there has been to Free Trade a sympathetic visual illusion in matters of faith as well as sight. Such has been the credulity of Englishmen.

It has been said that "a metaphorical expression, constantly repeated, little contradicted, is believed in by half-informed people." Doubtless, whatever a man hears or reads constantly without contradiction he is apt to believe.

It has been stated that an eminent translator of the Koran, by constantly poring over it, believed himself to have become a Mahometan. Likewise, with the perpetual repetition, without contradiction, of the phrase Free Trade. Unless Free Traders are individually convinced that their particular belief rests upon an assured foundation, their profession will not stand the *wearing test of experience ;* there must be reliable evidence that Free Trade exists as an intelligent and a *workable* principle.

In practice, the system has proved *un*workable, and England has suffered much as a great State by the loss of her bargaining power with other States, and also from her inability to bring about a commercial federation of the British Empire.

Loss of Bargaining Power.

Under a protective or tariff policy on the part of this country, in the place of the surrender or experiment of 1846, there would have been far greater likelihood of an approach on the part of foreign States to a free or fair exchange trade with us than has been the case under our present policy.

We should have realised, and given full effect to, a bargaining power commensurate with our vast and invaluable markets. It was an undoubted folly to throw these markets open to any single foreign State, let alone to all and sundry, without exacting guarantees, under a progressive reduction of embargoes, that we should receive fully equivalent privileges.

Premising, as we may do, simply for the sake of argument, that the economic conditions which European and other nations had arrived at, consequent upon the increase of population, and also due to improved productive appliances, demanded wider areas of trade exchanges for the more lucrative employment both of labour and capital, we may, without any difficulty, grant, that had Great Britain retained her independence in fiscal policy instead of throwing it away, the natural international demand of the middle of this century for those wider areas of trade exchange would have enabled Great Britain, by virtue of the value of her markets and her tariff policy, to have dictated to foreign States the terms upon which freer admission to our markets would be granted.

The tariff walls of foreign States at that time were for fiscal purposes mainly, and were not vexatiously protective. It is only since our surrender of our markets, without guarantees for reciprocity, and without compensating equivalents, that the fiscal tariff policy of these States has developed into a formidable and successful barrier of a protective character.

The various Royal Commissions and Parliamentary investigations and reports upon the depression of British trade are official and indirect proof that we have been *severely hit* by the growth of that foreign protective policy during the last thirty odd years.

The best that we have been able to do since the blunder of 1846 has been to give away one privilege and right of British citizenship after another in a vain expectation of satisfying the demand for more liberal treatment at the hands of foreign States. This I have dealt with in more detail in Chapter XIX. (pages 208-224).

It has been objected, on the part of the Free Traders, to the theory of bargaining power under a tariff policy, that no tangible benefit would be at all likely to accrue from it. In effect they say, " A protective policy would not assure Great Britain better terms or a better bargaining power in foreign markets, seeing that the tariffs of countries presently protective do not secure for these countries any better terms with each other than our Free Trade secures for us in the same markets."

This, no doubt, appears on the surface a fairly plausible statement ; against this, there is no answer possible to the averment made by the British Protectionist, that our Free Trade policy has secured for us no better terms than Protectionist countries enjoy from each other.

We have no compensation for the sacrifice we have voluntarily made of our valuable home and colonial markets. Whether Protection, and a return to a Protectionist policy, under movable tariffs, would or would not secure for Great Britain exceptional privileges in foreign markets, depends really upon the value and necessity to those foreign States of admission to the British markets.

The circumstances of the British Empire, and those of Protectionist foreign States, are not on all fours in this respect. Our persistence, without reciprocity, in a free import policy (of competing products only) has led during the past twenty or thirty years to the investment of our surplus capital more and more abroad, and to the increasing indebtedness and exploitation of certain foreign States and areas.

The consequence of all this is, that now the entire productive, banking, railway, and political systems of those States depends upon their continued use of the British market. They have been led on into obligations and developments, under which they are producing far above and beyond the possibilities of their own consumption, and any limitation of the freedom they enjoy of realising the value of that production would mean bankruptcy to those vast systems abroad, fostered by our Free Trade policy.

Any tariff we should impose upon such tributary foreign States, therefore, short of such effective limitation, would necessarily be paid by them, rather than they should lose our market; and one of the forms in which they would pay that price (in addition to the ordinary form of paying our tax upon their produce exported to us), would necessarily take the form of admitting British manufactures—if we demanded it— on lower terms than they would admit the manufac-

B

tures or similar produce of countries to whom they were similarly indebted.

But it is not true, however plausible it may appear, that Protectionist countries do not by virtue of these tariffs bargain to better advantage with each other than Great Britain has been able to do under her free import policy.

France, Germany, the United States of America, and every other Protectionist State, by virtue of their tariffs, do two very important things which we can not do because of our want of such a tariff policy.

In the first place, they reserve to their own home producers the preference and the first pull of their own markets, and thereby secure their industrial development against the desolating invasion of un-equal foreign competition. This security enables them to develop their multifarious or special in-dustries and advantages to the highest point of efficiency, with economy in production as the inevit-able result. (See Chapter XVI.)

In the second place, they distribute the burden of their taxation, their *war* debts and indemnities, the cost of erecting their railroads and public works, and of maintaining their fleets and armies, over the whole body of producers enjoying the privileges of their markets, with, if possible, the heavier proportion levied upon the enterprising outsider who demands and receives admission. By this means, their fiscal re-venues from tariffs lessen the burden and the pressure of their necessary taxation and expenditure upon their native producers and producing areas. Under our Free Trade policy, we in Great Britain paralyse home enterprise and industry by the devastating inroad of universal and subsidised foreign competition, and we lay the entire incidence of our local and imperial taxation absolutely as a burden upon our own land and labour, and the industrial products of the same.

The contrast, therefore, as to bargaining power is not to be taken simply in the form in which it has been ordinarily assumed by Free Traders, because foreign States actually do by their tariffs bargain better for their own subjects than Great Britain, without similar tariffs, is able to bargain for British subjects. But who can sufficiently estimate the renaissance to British home and imperial interests which would be bound to follow a return to fiscal sanity and the due consideration of the necessity to the foreigner of enjoying, even at a good price, the markets of the British Empire—which are to him so essential and so necessary.

CHAPTER II.

FOOLISH HOPES AND FALSE ISSUES.

The Nemesis of Wrong-doing—National Humiliation—Once
" Merrie England "—John Bull as he is "on view" to-day—
The Outlook Dark and Desperate—The Decay of British
Agriculture, in all its Branches, considered from a
National Standpoint—False Issues and False Remedies.

THE perplexities of nations, like the perplexities of
individuals, are in many instances the certain nemesis
of wrong-doing.

Nations, like individuals, err with a light heart, and
make haste to indefensible pursuits, and repent at
leisure. Nature does not allow a multitude of people
to sin with impunity, even when national folly is
made statutory, and the very temple of truth is
usurped and profaned by an established priesthood
of idolatry and prophets of error prophesying smooth
things and saying, " Peace, peace," when there is no
peace.

Nations are not above law ; the moral and ethical
law of God, denying to them, as to individuals, the
safe pursuit of falsehoods, covetousness, and injustice.

Sorrow and perplexity are sure to overtake the
Belshazzars' feast of national impiety, and the
suffering and perplexity are always the more intense
and appalling, because of the difficulty of getting a

nation to recant and to repent in a truly saving sense.

The false oracles continue enshrined long after their baneful influence has inflicted the inevitable curse, and the priests of falsehood, who live by the altar of apostacy and error, continue their witchcraft and sorcery long after events have condemned them and their works.   They still usurp their fatal influence and "heal the hurt of the daughter of my people slightly," so that an age of quackery succeeds the original transgression, and the exceeding bitterness of that transgression is brought home to the thresholds and the hearths of every class of the population.

There is no escape, and no evangel for national transgression short of national suffering and perplexity, and, if God will, national humiliation and repentance.

No one can say to-day of our country that it is happy.   Time was, when history and poetry spoke and sung, and with general truthfulness, of "Merrie England."   The lyrical echoes and reminiscences of past generations attest to the fact that *joy* was a frequent guest both of lordly hall and humble cottage, and that the occupations and the lives of the people were once brimful of mirth and happiness.   The joy and the sorrow of the people articulated itself in music and in song, with this marked characteristic, that the notes in the minor key were but few and far between, while deep diapasons of triumph and jocund interludes of delight thrilled the air of centuries.

It has remained for this *fin de siecle* (and that, the nineteenth of the Christian era) to witness the fading and dying away of every note and tone of national joy, the abandonment of all personifications for the nation implying triumph and delight, and the substitution for " Merrie England," for " Blest Albion," and for " Rule Britannia," of " John Bull," the unlovely epitome of worldly-mindedness and plethoric bovine stupidity.

No one will dispute a certain amount of magnitude, if not of grandeur and joy, to this ideal of the British people.   A sort of overgrown breeches-pocket personality, and sense and lust of the power of money, defines John Bull, the new and actual ideal of the British nation.   John Bull has acquired property, and lost juvenescence.   He has learned huckstering, and lost Arcady.   He has grasped the world with a bagman's avarice, and lost his yeoman and his patriot soul.

Usury and economic slavery are his theories of life, expressed in conditions of materialism and competition, and the disintegration and disestablishment of the ancient landmarks and organisations of society, as also, in the threatened dissolution of a vast growing and otherwise possible empire.

John Bull has made gods of his belly, his purse, and his business of changing money; and every institution of the times and seasons, and of means to ends, has been or is being altered and degraded to fit this contemptible confession of faith and ideal of existence.

We may very briefly review John Bull as he is at

present " on view " before humanity, with his plethoric and joyless possessions, and his multifarious interests and embarrassments.   One observation may be made of a prefatory character.   England is now known by civilised nations as the nation whose aged men and women of the common ranks are mostly miserable, and whose children of the same class have the least joy.   It must be a curse of terrible blight which permits or causes a great nation to go on with this disgraceful and unspeakable agony in its heart.   Yet this is now the first characteristic of our civilisation.

The expectation of life of our working men at forty-five years of age, and their prospects of independence after toiling with the best energy of their manhood, are now at their lowest actuarial estimation. Forty-five is a fatal and fateful climax of life to the toiling manhood of Great Britain.   From that point, there is a rapid economic effacement and displacement, and a decline to pauperism and the grave for those who have not been fortunate in a struggling lottery in which the blanks are very many and the prizes very very few.   There is no happy old age now for the British working-man, for peasant, artizan, or unskilled labourer, and this inevitable degradation and misery overtake the prudent and the virtuous, as well as the vicious and improvident.

It is this fact which makes the political outlook so dark and so desperate, because it is this generation alone which has reached the edge of the abyss in which national and social existence is engulfed.   There is a fearful prospect before the rising generation of this country, whose only present standing ground is

wrested from old age, and erected on the prostrate
bodies of their fathers.   Great Britain, in the event
of a successful blockade of the ports, or interception
of her shipping, could be starved into submission in
a week's time.

Great Britain has between two and three million
acres of fertile land, capable of supplying a higher
percentage of wheat per acre than the soils of foreign
States, gone out of cultivation, lying derelict in part,
and in part transformed into permanent pastures.
Great Britain is at the mercy of foreign States whenever a tempting occasion for any one or more of them
arises, and the national life is conducted under all
the fearful risks attendant upon this unparalleled
national folly.   It is not so very long ago in our history since the domestic supply of wheat was at least
two-thirds of the amount necessary for consumption,
leaving one-third to be derived from imports.

This state of matters was the maximum amount of
risk which statesmanship and patriotism should have
tolerated under any circumstances.   Now we grow
at home but about one-sixth, and are dependent upon
external supply for nearly five-sixths, the greater
proportion of which is from the United States of
America.

The "cheap loaf" is therefore dearly purchased
when the consequential damages and risks are duly
taken into account.   It so happens, however, that
France and Germany, who protect their agriculture
and arable areas by adequate fiscal duties, not only
maintain and even extend their cultivated areas, not
only save themselves from all the fearful risk and

much of the fearful cost of our fatuous policy, and
not only derive national revenue from the same, but
in the sequel enjoy at the same time, through their
protective policy, a cheaper loaf than so-called Free
Trade gives to Great Britain.   (See foot-note, Chapter
VII., page 89.)   The Free Trade swindle is, therefore,
in plain English, and practically, high protection to
foreign invested British capital, at the expense of the
fixed capital of this country, and the wages of the
working classes, which, in the end, bear the whole
weight of every public burden, when supply overtops
demand.

John Bull has created abundant perplexity for himself out of his folly.   His home farm is laid desolate
needlessly for the sake of his foreign investments, and
he loses, in large part, the capital value of the gifts
of Nature in the seasons, the fertile soil, the sunshine,
the productive labour, and the domestic exchanges
resulting from the annual golden harvest.

The purchasing power is regulated by the compara-
tive prosperity of the productive resources which are
being crippled, and, as a consequence, poverty and depression and blight result, population is displaced,
earnings are destroyed, and competition for employment is artificially stimulated—all leading to conflicts
of labour and capital and severe restrictions of
national production and profitable distribution.

Looking, in the first instance, at the experiences of
British and Irish agriculture under our most unwise
policy, the troubles and perplexities of John Bull are
manifold, vexatious, and to all appearances hopeless.
When the great industry and interests of wheat

cultivation were placed at the mercy of cheap ocean
transit of the world's surplusses of that commodity,
aggravated by the surrender of all fiscal regulation,
with a view to a bottom price and a living wage in
the matter of our greatest national industry, John
Bull's Free Trade advisers recommended him, with
a light heart, to "try something else."

It was supposed and asserted, with inexpressible
folly, that foreign competition would exhaust its
efforts in the supply of wheat, and that other and
subordinate agricultural products more suitable to our
soil and climate would still be left for the more
remunerative and lasting employment of the British
and Irish farmer. He was told—" Don't grow wheat
at all, if you can buy wheat you require cheaper from
abroad than you can grow it at home. Buy it from
the foreigner, and grind it and keep your mills going
at a better profit." But the British and Irish millers
were not very long in being given an object lesson in
the Free Trade they so much admired, by the arrival
of ocean cargoes of Minnesota flour—"golden fleece,"
"lily white," "five lilies," and other brands—the
Yankee building on the admirable foundation of our
free import policy and abolition of the Corn Laws,
by adding a little more labour to the exported commodity of wheat, by grinding it into flour for us, and
thus saving dollars in carriage, as well as displacing
more of John Bull's rural labour and fixed capital.
And here John Bull discovered a further lesson in
political economy which he might have foreseen, but
his blindness to which has cost him dearly. By
losing the grinding of so large a quantity of wheat

he lost the use for his subordinate agricultural pursuits of the bye products or "offals" of the same—so
invaluable for the economical breeding and feeding of
stock, *i.e.* cattle, pigs, and poultry, also the production
of three of the chief necessaries of life—meat, milk,
and   butter.   Thus,   when   the   same   Free   Trade
advisers of John Bull coolly counselled him to devote
his remaining energy in his remaining agriculture—
to the manufacture of beef, mutton, and pork—and
when, acting under this sublime counsel, he turned
some million acres of arable land into pasture, he
then discovered that he was placed at a great disadvantage with the Yankee and other foreigners in
the economical production of the same.   In due and
inevitable course—the flood-gates being opened, and
the industrial and economic defences levelled—the
beef, mutton, and pork—bacon and ham—enterprises
of John Bull were confronted by the import of similar
foreign products, more cheaply manufactured by the
foreigner.

Then, becoming a buyer of the foreign cattle in
competition with himself as a beef manufacturer, etc.,
conformable to the Free Trade policy, and the light
and leading of his brilliant Free Trade advisers, he
was shortly presented with the blessing of further
foreign competition by the advent of imports of dead
meat, frozen meat, tinned meat, meat essence, and
meat *ad. lib.*—all so much cheaper from foreign land
and labour sources than he was able to produce then
himself at home, even with the advantages of cheap
foreign wheat, flour, cattle, and so on.

An old, but by John Bull rather discarded, authority has said, with imperishable truth, that "a house divided against itself cannot stand, but cometh to naught." The house of John Bull is tumbling and crashing about his ears, because, as a speculative gambler and middleman in freely imported foreign produce, he has engaged more and more largely in business in competition with himself, and so undermined his ancient roof-tree and domestic fabric. Like a besotted fool, he has sought relief in the charms of Free Trade necromancy by taking hair after hair of the dog that has bitten him. With rapid strides in prodigal folly he has multiplied his perplexities and troubles, and descended into deeper and deeper degradation. Thus, abandoning one demolished industry after another, and ekeing out restricted resources of domestic employment of labour and capital with the aid of further foreign competition with himself, he bids fair to develop into a very vagrant and tramp, so far as industrial shelter and pursuit are concerned. His meat department is in economic ruin. His milk and butter department have no defence or immunity from the same fate. Already, and for some considerable time, Danish and other foreign butters—duty free, of course—have completely ousted him in respect to his rightful position in this part of his dairy business, leaving him only fag ends of inferiority, and a proportional turnover of no account to speak of. The dilapidation and poverty under which his limited agricultural pursuits are now carried on have placed him in an altogether inferior position as a producer, and the few —very few—things in which he is not yet assailed or supplanted by the foreigner are conducted at little or no profit to the department, because they are knocked out of their co-operative relationship to the whole system, which he ought to have retained under his own control.

The economy of agriculture is generally a unit, and cannot prosper when sub-divided and split into fractions. We have seen how the process of dis-integration began with the breaking down of the wheat-growing area, and the miserable surrender of the great staple and backbone of agricultural wealth and rural industry. Each subordinate industry was thereafter placed at an economic disadvantage, as Nature has denied to any country the possibility of prospering by despising her local bounties.

The economy of agriculture is a great unit, spreading out into multifarious branches, only if the great root and trunk of the system are conserved with jealous and protective care. Only fruitless and superfluous branches dare be lopped off, and that too only after their withered condition has sealed their doom ; but the trunk, never!

The idea of restricting the agricultural life and labour of a country of such developed and varied resources as the United Kingdom of Great Britain and Ireland to a fractional and crofter sub-division of petty agriculture is preposterous. Virgin territories of forest or prairie may begin their history by single efforts, each one of which, successfully pursued for a time, prepares the way for additional development, just as a tree in growing shoots out fresh branches. Thus, it is perfectly natural that

forest-land should develop into corn-land out of the
rich loam of the fallen and decayed leaves and under-
growth of centuries, and prairie-land and pasture
should, after being fertilised by flocks and herds,
develop into the cultivation of white crops, demanding and sustaining more human life and labour on the
soil, as population advanced and increased, giving
birth to hamlets, villages, and towns, and the urban
arts, and evoking those prosperous exchanges between town and country, by which the wealth of a
nation is created and increased for and by successive
generations. Thus does national life go forward in
development, and each part develops in multifarious
complexity in the beautiful co-operation of all parts
in a harmonious whole. All the talking of confining
the British farmer to jam, or flowers, or honey, or
milk, or potatoes, or butter, or cattle-raising on the
ruins of his arable cultivation, is retrogression, decay,
and certain death, if persisted in, because it is
inverting the order of nature, and invoking the curse
upon national folly and crime, instead of the blessing
upon national wisdom and virtue.

The political economy of Free Trade is stamped
with the lie—it is branded with infamy and falsehood
by the unerring and inexorable hand of Nature, whose
order this covetous and mammon-worshipping monster
has despised and inverted. Give up wheat, British
farmer, give up farming in the fullest sense, bucolic
yeoman John Bull, and entrench yourself in the last
ditch of gooseberries, briars, and brambles, and jam !
Oh, what cruel nonsense ! Wheat is the crown and
climax of agricultural economy, the glory and neces-

sity of good husbandry and the husbandman. Whether John Bull wills it or knows or believes it or not, if he gives up and loses his wheat growing, he gives up and loses all, for Nature denies him the possibility of prospering in any of the subordinate branches thereafter.

To follow up the perplexities of John Bull, resulting immediately from the false political economy of Free Trade, is an almost endless exercise and study; but one or two salient and present-day additional and consequential aspects must yet be noted. Even to enumerate these in their natural and chronological order would be useful, but the subject demands a little more than this. The reader is referred to Chapter XV.—"The Fate of Being Undeceived"—for the most part for a description of the ruinous extension of the results of free import folly to the textile and other manufacturing industries, the condition of the working classes under universal and unreciprocated foreign competition, the transfer of British capital and machinery abroad, and the consequent depression and decay in our export trade and command of external markets. In what remains of this chapter the reader is invited to consider the perplexed and troubled condition of John Bull, unwilling to admit his error and folly, laying the blame on anything but the true cause, and insanely devising and endeavouring to apply quack and contradictory remedies.

The first marked perplexity in this respect is the political one expressed in the demand, under the meaningless term " Home Rule," for the breaking up of our partial imperial unity into autonomous parts.

The extension of the county franchise to the illiterate
and priest-ridden peasantry of Ireland—the greatest
victim and sufferer by our Free Trade folly—brought
this distinctly into the region of so-called practical
politics.   But this is really but a development of
the tendency under the popular unrest and suffering
induced by Free Trade to alleviate and remedy social
misery by organic changes.   The children cry for
bread and the party politician offers them a stone.
They ask for an egg and they receive a scorpion.
Thus, in circumstances of national decadence and
misfortune, the Imperial Government relieves itself of
sorrowful responsibility, multiplies local authorities
and increases taxation enormously and generally.

There is no essential harm in political devolution
any more than in technical education, but these are
only blessings when they fit in with the strong and
healthy existence and growth of the existing order,
the change being always properly a constructive, but
never a destructive devolution.

Technical education and local government, plus
all we ought to build up and retain in vital energy,
in imperial solidarity and unity, and security of
markets for our producers, are good ; but they are no
substitutes for these, and no cures whatever for the
evils occasioned by the want of them.   In the region
of political perplexity of John Bull, we have further
to notice the internecine and confiscatory character
of other schemes of re-adjustment and relief.

The popular agitation and the official promises
and strategic equivocations about the landed proprietors, the Established Church endowments, ac-

quisition by the State of mining royalties, and
suppression of public-houses without compensation—
all occupying along with other miserable and conten-
tious topics the public mind, while trade and empire
are threatened with ruin, are conspicuous examples
of the perplexities and troubles of John Bull in his
false and ludicrous and sorrowful position.

Taxes which ought to be raised by fiscal duties for
imperial and local purposes are to be otherwise
raised, or provided by a system of oppression and
plunder, for the sake of sparing the fetish of Free
Trade—as if its victims were not enough already.
All the while, the political and social current is
violently contradicting the Free Trade policy in
other respects in organised exclusive dealing, or
boycots on a large scale, and statutory regulations,
repressions and inspections of an *internal* character,
demanded by the demoralising results of an intoler-
able competition in every business.

How funny it must be to a disinterested outsider
to see John Bull grovelling before his fetish of Free
Trade, and yet demanding to be tied up with cords
and manacles amid the gymnastics of his *self-wound-
ing* and *self-mutilating paroxysms.*

Not less interesting than the political and social
perplexities which we have been considering are the
financial troubles and problems which have also been
of late distracting John Bull. I shall have very
little difficulty in placing these in the category of the
foolish hopes and false issues which are, in part, the
theme of this chapter.

That these financial troubles, with their attendant

quack remedies, should exist at all, is largely the consequence of our fiscal system, and a blind and ob-
stinate adherence to it in spite of presages and warnings. We have reached a period when, even after
the interest upon the consolidated national debt has
been reduced, to match the reduced earnings and
profits of production, the accumulations of unused
capital at the Bank of England and other banks, and
the low rate of interest upon deposits, has become
alarming.

No explanation of a satisfactory nature is possible
for this which does not involve the consideration of
our fiscal policy as false and mischievous and illusory.
If the pretensions and prognostications of Free Trade
political economy could be justified, this would not—
in the absence of other extraordinary circumstances—
be the case.

There are abundant objects in public and repro-
ductive expenditure, municipal and otherwise, as well
as of private industrial and commercial venture, to
employ every available farthing, if only the two
things of which we have been robbed by Free Trade,
namely, security and certainty of profit, existed.
There ought to be, and might be, a continuous extension and renewal of dwellings and townships, in
keeping with increasing population. Railways and
waterways to connect our vast, various, and distant
producing areas with each other for effective and
economic connection with markets, and an expansion
of industrial and productive enterprise, are all abundantly called for. But finance does not respond to
all this till demand and desire are authorised by

public confidence—the very thing which John Bull
in his Free Trade frenzy has destroyed.

It is not under the sequences of a system of exploitation, and with a bankrupt vista of profitless
endeavour, that financial prosperity can be stimulated
and commanded.

In the dilemma contrived for John Bull by Free
Trade, in these circumstances, as in the political and
social aspects, the remedy is recommended of robbing
the public creditor by juggling with the currency.
Confiscation reappears in the financial world, in the
proposals of the Free Trade bi-metallists, to confer
an artificial value to an unlimited degree to the commodity of silver (mainly produced by the foreigner)
by giving it a fixed legal value in relation to gold,
irrespective of its commercial value ; and this proposal comes from the very party which denies to
our great wheat-growing interest even the smallest
amount of fiscal justice, let alone Protection, and who
traverse land and sea to make proselytes to the proposition that a preferential trade policy for the
British Empire is impracticable, and can never be.
There is great confusion of mind and perplexity in
all this.

It is not within the scope of this chapter to deal
exhaustively with the silver question, but one or two
further observations may, at least, be made. First,
upon the fluctuations in the rate of exchange between
silver and gold-using countries as a plea for the protection of silver.

Commercially looked at, the question may here be
asked—Why cannot the difference or depreciation of

value of silver in exchange for gold be calculated in the contracts, or made a subject of insurance, or otherwise dealt with ? If Free Trade had been what its advocates claimed, we would have had fiscal and monetary unity possible over all our Empire. If Free Trade had fulfilled its promises, the producer, selling at a gold price or on a gold basis in a silver-using country, would have been enabled safely to discount the depreciation of silver in the price obtainable for his goods ; the Anglo-Indian official would have done the same with contracts as to salary, and the Indian Government would have had no difficulty in covering the gold premium in its remittances home out of its surplus revenues. But Free Trade has blighted the finance of the Government of India. Free Trade has transferred British capital and machinery to Oriental areas in competition with ourselves at home. Free Trade, in its absurd manifestations, has upset every calculation in business, and common sense might determine that Free Trade, not the currency, needs reforming.

Secondly, as to re-adjusting the ratio between the silver and the gold coinage. If, when the legal ratio of 15½ of silver to 1 of gold was fixed, this ratio was conformable to the commercial relation of these precious metals to each other, and now, on account of greater activity in silver production, the commercial ratio is 21 to 1, why should not the legal ratio for silver as a limited legal tender be raised to the same point, with the *requisite addition* of *weight* to all future silver coins, and the old coins, of the old ratio, be called in at the banks ?

In this matter, as in the others treated of in this chapter, John Bull is assuredly chasing another of the Will-o'-the-wisps with which the Free Trade morass is so populous.

Free Trade, delusively beautiful to his enamoured imagination at first sight, has fooled him long enough. While he has still strength left, and is not altogether and hopelessly bewildered and benighted, let him dis-card the baneful practice.

BEWARE!

" I know a maiden fair to see,
        Take care !
She can both false and friendly be,
        Beware !   Beware !
        Trust her not,
She is fooling thee.

" She gives thee a garland woven fair,
        Take care !
It is a fool's-cap for thee to wear,
        Beware !   Beware !
        Trust her not,
She is fooling thee."

CHAPTER III.

CAPITAL AND LABOUR.

The Relations of Labour and Capital as expressed by " Orthodox " Political Economy—The Competition of Individuals
the Modern Basis of Trade—The Gospel of Individualism
—Two Great Events in Europe—Political Economy Relegated to Jupiter and Saturn—Capital, its Rights and Obligations in regard to Land and Labour—Labour has a Lieu
upon Capital—Under "Free Trade," Capital is Divorced
from Alliance with Labour, and from the Soil—Under
Protection, Capital is compelled to assist Labour and the
Commonwealth—Protective Relations with the Colonies—
An Equitable Reciprocity—Mr. Medley's "Selfish National
Point of View."

THE orthodox political economy which got established during the beginning of this century, and which
is breaking down during its later years, endeavoured
to systematise on a new basis, and with new defini-
tions, the relations of labour and capital.

The basis of the reasoning of that school was that
of selfishness and individualism, and, as a system, it
was really the grand ethical discovery of the philosophers of atheism and of the French Revolution, in
the chaos which followed the disruption of society and
destruction of institutions in France at that period.

With all its affectation of enlightenment, it was
really a relapse into paganism and barbarism, and

38

with all its wild and dramatic appeals to liberty, it was really a system whose logical outcome ensured the economic slavery of nations, and of the non-propertied classes.

It made competition—the competition of individuals—the basis of society and of trade, and it founded this, again, on the monstrous induction that the only constant and dependable motive of human nature was, is, and would ever be, selfishness.

In effecting the disruption of the old order, its new gospel of liberty and individualism was a balance of selfishness established by competition, secured by liberty of the strong to devour the weak, and realised by the subjection of the weaker to the stronger, and the ultimate survival of the fittest—in this savage sense.

The theory and the system had its attractions to the bourgeoisie—to the middle classes, who saw in its acceptance by populations the guarantee of the break up of all reciprocal obligation between class and class, between property and poverty, and between capital and labour.

Two great events in Europe prevented its complete acceptance, with all its delusive and glittering attractions, its sordid appeals to covetousness, and its reassertion of the doctrine of Cain, " Am I my brother's keeper ? " The first consisted in the enfranchisement in France, and also in Germany at a later period, of a sufficiently large proportion of the population in the possession of the soil ; and the second, in the organisation of labour in Great Britain on a protective basis—in other words, of British

Trade Unionism.[1] These two institutions—the peasant proprietary of France and Germany, and the Trade Unionism of Great Britain, are essentially social and national, protective and not competitive, and their growth and development have prevented the desolating triumph of materialistic cosmopolitanism.

They keep alive to-day, in spite of the bourgeoisie doctrines of supply and demand and of *laissez-faire*, an unconscious appeal to Socialism, Conservatism, and Nationalism, and to the economic ideas antecedent to those which are now considered orthodox. As a consequence we have the Protectionist policy of every democracy whose soil is owned largely by the people. We have the doctrine of the " minimum wage," and the principle of judicial rents, all of which fly in the face of so-called political economy, and relegate it to Jupiter and to Saturn.

It is to the old political economy, and not to the new, that labour has ever to make its appeal and the cultivator of the soil has still to look, in order that national society and humanity may survive the encroachments and the ravages of competition stimulated by irresponsible capital.

And here I will state in a popular form what constitutes capital, and what are its rights and obligations in regard to land and labour. Capital is the stored-up results of labour. It is unconsumed value of previous production expressed in documents of credit and of money. It represents the savings of production over consumption, and becomes, as a

[1] John Bright did not love Trade Unionism.

property, a lien upon labour. It commands the purchase and supply of commodities and service necessary to its own conservation and reproduction.

It is all the while the result of previous labour; and, as civilisation and society become less primitive, it is the result of the operation jointly of previous capital and labour, allied together in production.

In nature, therefore, if not in law, labour has a lien upon capital quite as much as capital has upon labour; and the distinguishing difference between Free Trade and Protection consists simply and solely in this, that Free Trade confers upon the capitalist the right of going past his national partner, and buying labour where it is cheapest, irrespective of kindred, of country, of religion, or locality, or any social bond or obligation whatsoever; while Protection ensures that the labour of the locality and the country shall have a secure lien upon the capital, or unconsumed product of its previous exertion.

But at this point I come to the distinction between one form of capital and another.

There is the fixed capital of property, and the floating or fluid capital of money.

Money is a later development of the savings of production over consumption, and is expressive of conditions which remove the barter of commodity for commodity, and of goods for goods, or of time for time, farther and farther away from the original transaction.

In all nations the first investment of capital has been in land; secondly, in other tools of production, and of distribution, which may include buildings,

roads, machinery, ships, docks, etc.; and, thirdly,
monetary documents representing the surplus-value
or accumulated product of production and exchange.

A point is reached when accumulation ceases to be
absorbed in property of a fixed and determinate
character within the State, and when, in the form
solely of money—of documents of credit and obligation and coin—a circulating medium and an instru-
ment of external investment is thus created.

By the laws of usury and the institution of banking, this form of capital becomes available as a further
stimulus to industry and an extension of the relations
of labour and capital.

Under Free Trade, this fluid capital is entirely
divorced from alliance with labour, that is, with the
labour of the country, which presumably has a lien
upon it for employment. It is divorced from alliance
with the soil, and the institutions of the land where
it derived, in partnership with native labour, its
earning power.

Under Protection, it is compelled to continue its
assistance to labour and the commonwealth, and to
obtain its reproduction only in this way. All its exchanges must, under Protection, reproduce and replace
another capital at home, and give employment to
native labour.

This does not presuppose the exclusion of foreign
trade, but it distinctly presupposes and determines
that the productions imported from abroad must be
also exchanged for productions of native labour, and
that their cost shall not be liquidated out of capital
apart from that labour.

By a system of colonisation, and of *protective relations with these colonies*, an outlet is derived for surplus capital and surplus labour, in an artificial extension of the imperial area; and this protective relation carries forward into this new area the harmonious reciprocity of alliance and obligation between the capital of the country and the labour of its non-propertied classes.

By a fiscal regulation of exports, and of imports also, Protection assures, in respect to foreign trade, an equitable reciprocity and a mutually advantageous balance of trade. But where the middle and monied classes interested in traffic and in foreign investment are given a free and unregulated import of commodities, and use of the home market for such, not only are our more distant colonies sacrificed to the advantage of foreign States, but our labour is deprived of its lien upon capital, and the security and certainty of its employment in competition with the surplus labour and surplus labour products of the outside world.

The effect of this is to increase the difficulties of agriculture, and of all employment within the country. The surplus capital, which, under a wise Protection, would go to our colonies, would invite thence our enterprising yeomen and younger sons generally. The competition for farms at home would be less cruel and unreasonable, while the area of profitable cultivation for secure markets would be more extended. The emigration of our surplus population would follow the movements of our surplus capital, and the pressure of competition in the labour market in our towns would be reduced, while the demand for all effective labour would be increased.

This would not, of course, suit our Free Trade friends, who live on the congestion of labour at home, on the earnings of foreign investment, and the profit derived from the import of foreign surplusses into our markets.

So long as our farmers and working classes can continue to struggle under economic slavery and exclusive taxation, so long will these parasites glory in the humbug and delusion which they impose on the national intelligence under the spurious title of Free Trade.

Their views and aims are vastly different, as the following extract from Mr. George W. Medley's " The Reciprocity Craze " will show :—

" There are good reasons for supposing that the existing state of things is not to be regretted by us from the selfish national point of view.

" I am not sure, as some are, that Great Britain would in the long run be a gainer by universal Free Trade, and I now start this as a question worthy of calm discussion.

" If universal Free Trade existed, its vital and energetic principle, division of labour, would, of course, have full play, and mankind would by its means achieve the maximum of protection at the minimum of cost.

" I am not quite certain that, as a nation, we should, under it, be absolutely or comparatively as well off as we are now.

" Let us for a moment imagine all hostile tariffs suddenly abolished.

" Has anyone ever seriously considered the possible effects, immediate or remote, which might arise ? Among them would be :—

" 1. A sudden and vast demand for labour at home.

" 2. A sudden and great increase in wages.

" 3. A rapid increase in the number of our factories, workshops, mills, furnaces, etc.

" 4. A rampant speculation in everything connected with trade and manufactures.

" 5. A general rise in prices distressful to those with fixed incomes.

" 6. A rush of population from home and abroad to our manufacturing centres.

" 7. A stimulus given to marriage and population.

" 8. A demoralisation of our labouring classes.

" 9. Strikes for an increase of wages.

" 10. The culmination of the foregoing.

" 11. The beginning of a reaction, owing to the commencement of foreign competition.

" 12. The commencement of a fall in prices."

What have British citizens to say to this ?

CHAPTER III.—*Continued.*

TAXATION A BURDEN UPON NATIVE INDUSTRY.

Capital Assisting Foreign Labour to Supplant Native Labour—
Free Trade makes Labour a Cosmopolitan Commodity ;
Distresses Labour by an Artificially Stimulated Supply and
an Artificially Depressed Demand—Labour and Capital in
Industrial Partnership—Local and Imperial Taxation a
Charge on the Labour of this Country—Restrictive Legisla-
tion—The Workman's Interest in Cheapness an Illusory
Dream—Depreciating the *Capital of Labour*—The "Cheap-
Loaf" Fraud has its Historical Counterpart in the Esau
Transaction—A Free Trade Proletariat Abasing Itself be-
fore the Fetish of Universal Competition, only Paralleled by
the Baal Worshippers of Old—Blinded and Bound Samson.

IT is very obvious, from the considerations submitted
in the previous chapter, that labour has a vital interest in at least two aspects of its relations with capital
which the Free Trade policy is at variance with, and
the conditions of which can only be insured under a
policy of *wise* Protection.

These are, first, the continued alliance or partnership of labour with capital ; and, secondly, the interest
of labour in the ultimate product of their *joint*
exertions.

We have seen that Free Trade, in its essence, is the
removal of the tie between the capitalist and the
native producer in the matter of the employment of
labour, since, by the policy of free imports, that

capital can be engaged more and more in substituting foreign labour for native labour, and thereby creating a glut in the labour market. Every shipload of foreign production in manufactured articles, or in any products whatever proper to the labour of the country, represents in a concrete form the introduction of so much more competition into our industrial life, equal to the number of foreign labourers and skilled workmen necessary to their production.

Free Trade transforms the co-ordinate relations of capital and labour into hostile relations, and makes labour in its relations to capital merely a cosmopolitan commodity, to be bought in the cheapest market and to be dispensed with when a cheaper can be had.

Every effort which, under these circumstances, is made by labour to secure terms and humane conditions, apart from fiscal protection, is necessarily abortive, and simply operates as a premium upon more extensive foreign investment of British capital, and more extensive importation of competing labour products.

Free Trade, in the British sense, that is, free import from whatever quarter, and apart altogether from reciprocity, is a pledge to all such foreign investment and speculation in foreign land and labour products that these commodities shall reach our markets and enter into our consumption, whatever happens to our local areas and native dependent population, and that, meanwhile, under the pressure of this external competition, capital shall have the advantage of the distresses of labour through the operation of *arti-*

ficially stimulated supply and artificially depressed demand.

It is, therefore, a policy of high Protection to capital, and especially to commercial capital and the " middleman " class, operating upon, not the partnership, but the *subjection* and *humiliation of labour.*

Under a sufficiently effective fiscal protection, the relations of supply to demand could be regulated in favour of the equitable interests of labour and capital in industrial partnership, and in favour of labour in any case, since the demands of luxury and of consumption in every form for commodities would, necessarily, be compelled to employ native labour, and, on that labourer's own terms.

It would matter very little to the working classes how the wealth of the country in the shape of rents and profits should in the course of events be invidiously distributed, if its ultimate reproduction and employment in consumption, from the building and furnishing of palaces and residences, to the clothing, feeding, and serving and general supply of commodities for the rich as well as the poor, necessarily demanded the employment of *native labour.*

It would further matter very little to the same labouring classes what amount of foreign production should even then enter into our imports, if every such import necessitated an export of equal value which constituted a necessary demand upon employment at home.

Free Trade, as it exists with us, not only makes no provision for this, but provides that it may be dispensed with altogether, and holds out to nations who rigorously tax or exclude our products, the free and continued use of our vast markets, upon which native labour *has the first claim.*

Protection alone can secure this market, in the first instance, as the lucrative and secure property of the native workman.

Consider, therefore, how labour is robbed and fooled under this system. First, in the matter of taxation: all our imperial and local taxation is *a burden upon our native industry,* and every item which is a product of British and Irish labour can only enter our market, or the market of the foreigner, after it has borne its proportion of this taxation as a part of its oncost. (The only exception to this is in the case of exciseable manufactures, which have a " drawback " on export equal to the duty at home.) If, therefore, the local and imperial taxation, which is estimated at about 20 per cent. of the value, is a part and proportion of the oncost on all our home production, the free import of the foreign is protected to the extent of that exemption in competition with it in *our* markets, subject only to the cost of freight and extra handling. But even this hypothetical advantage is sacrificed under the modern conditions of transit and the preferential terms accorded to foreign imports.

How can labour prevent capital from extorting the whole of this out of actual or possible wages when labour is deprived of its lever through the glut of supply over demand which is the result of the external competition ?

The same observations apply with equal force and

D

truth to all restrictive legislation at home on our factories, ships, and workshops.

If capital, which otherwise would have to hire labour subject to these restrictions, can employ the labour of countries where these restrictions do not operate, it can then by the law of supply and demand escape the incidence both of the taxation and the restrictions, and transfer their incidence entirely upon labour. This it does. This is just what happens. When once the competition for employment is artificially and unduly stimulated, as it is under this Free Trade policy, then labour has, eventually, to bear every burden, and to suffer the economic result of every restriction which, in its blindness, it intended should fall upon capital alone. Nay, it may be further stated, that every economic and social adjustment intended afterwards to ameliorate the social condition of labour will be by economic sequence confiscated by capital and sacrificed by labour under the dire exigencies of competition resulting from the Free Trade policy.

The second element of vital interest to labour, and which only a policy of wise Protection can ensure, is the interest of labour in the value of the product of its exertions *jointly* with capital.

This element, it may here be remarked, is only now being recognised by labour, and that under the pressure of economic distress.

The workman's interest in cheapness is a very illusory dream in the end, as the depreciation of prices, simply as a result of competition, spells, inexorably and logically, low wages and precarious employment. So long, as from circumstances which were purely adventitious, under our Free Trade policy, we enjoyed " brisk trade " and big demand for labour, labour disregarded its ultimate interest in the market-value of its productions, and founded upon the demand, the temporary demand, for labour alone. It dreamed of erecting a minimum price for labour while denying a minimum price for commodities, the product of labour. It blandly and blindly witnessed the exploitation of areas and resources in the mad pursuit of a plethora—mad, because it overlooked the fact of its *vital interest* in the *conserved value* of *its own exertions* and *its own heritage.*

Who benefits by the plethora accompanied by the *degradation of labour?* Those who are capitalists alone. Those who are consumers and not producers. Those who toil not and spin not, but who live as parasites on industry, on the earnings of transferable investments.

Every depreciation of prices, the result of competition, depreciates the *capital of labour,* and appreciates the capital of idleness and speculation.

This is the essence of the "cheap loaf" fraud, which has its historical counterpart in the barter by Esau of his priceless birthright for the miserable mess of pottage.

The demand for Protection is, and will be, the demand of the intelligent proletariat. The upper and the trading classes can and do make the Free Trade policy fit their interests, however it may conflict with their individual humanity and patriotism.

A Free Trade proletariat abasing itself before the

fetish of universal competition is only paralleled by
the Baal worshippers of old vainly calling on their
Baal to hear and to help them.

A Free Trade proletariat enduring the economic
slavery of the system is the spectacle repeated in the
nineteenth century of the blinded and bound Samson
the sport of the lords of the Philistines, and portends
the appropriate catastrophe of a social cataclysm.

CHAPTER IV.

PRODUCTION THE SOURCE OF NATIONAL WEALTH —THE SUPERIORITY OF HOME TRADE.

Labour Applied to the Cultivation of the Soil, and upon the Pro-
ducts of the Soil—The Two Modes of Wealth Creation—Quo-
tations from the Free Traders' Economic Bible—Home
Trade—The Replacement of Capital—Two Home Products
Exchanged at Home means that the Nation Gains the Entire
Revenue of these Products—Revenue Primary, Expenditure
Secondary—Everybody's Industry would Further and Help
the Industry of Everybody else—The Reduplicative Opera-
tion of the Home Trade—The Liberty of Every Man to
" Do " his Neighbour—The Great Kingdom—" A Glasgow
Lesson in Free Trade "—An Economic Absurdity—Learned
Professors and High Priests holding Briefs for the Cobden
Club: Aerial Food of Abstract Principles and Theories—The
" Parable of Labour."

ALL economists agree that the original source of all
wealth is the soil.

The cultivation of the soil is the means of subsist-
ence for the labourer, and not only so, but whatever
the soil yields in excess of the needs of the actual
cultivators, is an increase of the existing stock.   Thus
the labour applied upon the soil differs from the
labour applied to the productions of the earth, for
the latter can only add to the material worked upon
a value exactly equal to that expended during the
execution of the work.

This important difference in the two modes of

wealth creation is well worth keeping in mind *when England's population is constantly increasing, and her power of food production is continuously decreasing.*

Chapter II. of this book refers to the decay of British agriculture, and deals very fully with this subject, but the writer considers it desirable to place before his readers certain statements of Adam Smith bearing upon the value of the cultivation of the soil :—

" Wealth of Nations," B. II., Chapter V., we read : " No equal capital put into motion a greater quantity of productive labour than that of the farmer. Not only his labouring servants, but his labouring cattle, are productive labourers. In agriculture, too, Nature labours along with man ; and though her labour costs no expense, its produce has its value as well as that of the most expensive workmen. . . . . It is the work of Nature which remains, after deducting or compensating everything which can be regarded as the work of man. *No equal quantity of productive labour employed in manufactures can ever occasion so great reproduction.* In them Nature does nothing ; man does all ; and the reproduction must always be in proportion to the strength of the agents that occasion it. The capital employed in agriculture, therefore, not only puts into motion a greater quantity of productive labour than any equal capital employed in manufactures ; but, in proportion, too, to the quantity of productive labour which it employs, it adds a much greater value to the annual produce of the land and labour of the country, to the real wealth and revenue of its inhabitants. Of all the ways in which a capital can be employed, it is by far the most advantageous to society."

Let the reader mark, learn, and inwardly digest these extracts from the Free Traders' Economic Bible—pertaining to the greatest industrial interest of the nation. Those who support our bogus Free Trade in their superior wisdom affect with a light heart to totally disregard the supreme value, and discount even the existence of this perennial source of national wealth. These imperishable lines of Adam Smith should rebuke all who would sacrifice our national agriculture, and lower the exchangeable value of all our produce.

We may pass on from the consideration of the cultivation of the soil (to add anything to the quotation from Adam Smith is to gild refined gold), and review other forms of production. The products of the soil have to be prepared for the use of man, and this provides employment to various classes of labour : the reaper, the miller, the baker—all these labour as well as the plougher and the sower.

The labour of the weaver supplements that of the grower of flax ; the grower of wool gives place to those who convert the wool into cloth ; the breeder and feeder of cattle to the tanner ; and so an indefinite amount of labour is employed from one process to another. Each product gains a value precisely equal to the labour expended. Now, it is evident, that the whole value of a commodity is spent in its production, and yet re-appears in the shape of the new product. That in its production there is an expenditure not of the profit merely, but of the entire value.

It is this expenditure which gives revenue to the community, and creates a demand and market for the various products of labour; in fact, *establishes domestic exchanges.*

We may pass under review the whole range of native productions—agricultural or manufactured— and it is evident that the values denote the creation of national wealth.

We see that the earth furnishes the means of wealth, but labour and industry connects and combines the various productions of the soil for use and consumption ; labour is the universal agent in the creation of wealth—a power of which man is the machine—capable under human intelligence and industry of indefinite development. A great deal could be here said respecting the perfecting of the productive powers of labour—mechanical inventions, and the division of labour. The operations of labour increase when the number of those employed augment in proportion to the increasing number of consumers; consumers multiply as the result of an increase of capitals—the revenues secured in the various branches of industrial production.

These reflections lead to the consideration of the second part of my subject, namely, the superiority of home trade or domestic exchanges, compared with foreign trade and foreign exchanges.

For a definition of home trade I turn again to the Free Traders' Koran :—" The capital which is employed in purchasing in one part of the country in order to sell in another the produce of the industry of that country, generally replaces by such operation two distinct capitals that had both been employed in the agriculture or manufacture of that country, and thereby enables them to continue that employment. . . . . When *both* are the produce of domestic industry, it necessarily replaces, by every such operation, *two distinct capitals*, which had *both* been employed in supporting productive labour, and thereby enables them to continue that support. The capital which sends Scotch manufactures to London, and brings back English manufactures and corn to Edinburgh, necessarily replaces, by every such operation, *two British capitals*, which had *both* been employed in the agriculture or the manufactures of *Great Britain*. The capital employed in purchasing foreign goods for home consumption, when this purchase is made with the produce of domestic industry, replaces, too, by every such operation, two distinct capitals, but *one of them only* is employed in supporting domestic industry. The capital which sends British goods to Portugal, and brings back Portuguese goods to Great Britain, replaces by every such operation *only one British capital*. The other is a Portuguese one. Though the returns, therefore, of the foreign trade of consumption should be as quick as those of the home trade, the capital employed in it will give but ONE HALF THE ENCOURAGEMENT TO THE INDUSTRY OR PRODUCTIVE LABOUR OF THE COUNTRY. . . . . A capital, therefore, employed in the home trade will sometimes make twelve operations, or be sent out and returned twelve times, before a capital employed in the foreign

trade of consumption has made one. IF THE
CAPITALS ARE EQUAL, THEREFORE, THE ONE WILL
GIVE FOUR-AND-TWENTY TIMES MORE ENCOURAGE-
MENT AND SUPPORT TO THE INDUSTRY OF THE
COUNTRY THAN THE OTHER."

The replacement of capital referred to by Adam
Smith clearly means that when two home products
are exchanged at home the producing nation gains
the entire revenue of those products ; that the nation
is so much richer ; "for, while producing, it spends the
entire gross value, and, nevertheless, after it has produced, it yet has the entire gross value left in another
shape."

The purchase of foreign commodities (for home
consumption) by the sale of British commodities implies that you have the value and the market of *one*
industry only. We may well exclaim if such be the
consequences where there is reciprocity! What are
the consequences under the sort of Free Trade which
England is experiencing to-day? From these facts
it follows of necessity that, to allow foreign trade to
displace home trade is very *bad* policy; and consequently that a policy of Protection to home industry
is the true policy of a country.[1]

Under free competing imports the Britons' industry is superseded by the industry of the foreigner,
but under a wise protective system in Great Britain
and Ireland, "everybody's industry would further and

---

[1] The devastating consequences of our system are to be found
in the table of statistics appended to Chapter XIV. of this volume,
" Protection to British and Irish Labour."

help the industry of everybody else." We should have a double set of producers, double production of wealth, and a double set of home markets, insured by the "reduplicative operation of the home trade." Agriculture, mining, and manufactures making up a framework of industry, self-supporting, and ministering to the comfort of the whole community and the stability of the State.

Increasing the volume of national production will alone bring comfort and happiness to our people. The life of trade depends upon it, and so does the wealth of the nation. Pursue for another generation the policy of cheapness at any cost, and England's wealth of every kind will vanish like Aladdin's palace.

As it is, each individual is supposed to be occupied with his own concerns ; supervision and control is resented as an interference with natural liberty—the liberty of every man to " do " his neighbour—resulting in confusion and misery. Personal liberty is that every man should buy in the cheapest market regardless of consequences ; ideas of justice and equity are determined by prices ; there is no thought of the empire as *one commonwealth*, reserving a preferential market for its own productions, so that the community can gain in revenue. There is no thought of the great kingdom, which includes the interests of both the consumer and the producer : buy the cheaper foreign commodity and ignore the home and colonial producer and all the industrial classes of the country. This is the recommendation of the *laissez-faire* philosophy.

Free Trade regards the expenditure of the individual, and disregards the revenue of the nation.

The purchase of cheaper foreign commodities to supercede home productions is no gain but a loss to the nation, because it destroys national income.

No argument is needed to show that under unrestricted competition the prices of all productions must fall, and fall to the lowest level; with prices, profits must similarly fall; with profits, wages; and with all these three, the interest or remuneration of capital to the lowest level.

A Glasgow Lesson in Free Trade.

Under this heading the writer, in the autumn of 1893, engaged in an interesting controversy with the editor of the *Manchester City News.* The subject under discussion was the purchase of German steel rails and fish-plates for the Glasgow tramways by the City Council. By giving the contract to Germany, Glasgow gained £288, and lost £5,127. My opponent replied to my analysis of the transaction by saying: "An argument, to be sound, should stand a little stretching. Instead of there being only a difference of £288, or five per cent. against the Glasgow rail-makers, let us suppose there was 100 per cent.—that the Glasgow people required £12,800 for the rails and fish-plates, which could be procured in Germany for £5,400. Would Mr. Burgis say the order must be given to the Glasgow firm? Of course he would. And if the Glasgow firm wanted £25,000 for their goods, all the more reason for giving them the order.

Would not the £25,000 be revenue to be spent in Glasgow? A moment's consideration of Mr. Burgis' argument will show to what absurd positions it will lead to."

The writer rejoined:—

" Under these conditions named, I say the order should *not* be given to the Glasgow makers. There is no absurdity in purchasing a domestic commodity which is dearer—and even considerably dearer—than the foreign. The absurdity consists in paying such an excess as is *unjustifiable on economic grounds.* If the nation pays 50 per cent. more for the domestic than for the foreign, it still clears a profit of 50 per cent. by the transaction; if it pays 90 per cent. more, it clears a profit of 10 per cent.; if it pays 100 per cent. more, then the account is balanced, and it neither gains or loses. There is no absurdity in the City of Glasgow Council having the rails and fish-plates produced in Glasgow at a cost of £5,415, when the same can be produced from Germany for £288 less money; but it is absurd for the City Council, by giving the contract to Germany, to cause the city, and nation, to lose £5,127 in revenue to save £288 in expenditure. The City Council is simply dreaming of an imaginary gain, while it inflicts upon itself a loss of 95 per cent. The absurdity actually begins after the domestic commodity has become 100 per cent. dearer than the foreign, when the nation begins to lose rather more in expenditure than it earns in revenue. I cannot stretch the argument beyond 100 per cent., as you assume, but I have stretched it a good deal. I am interested in seeing if you can demon-

strate the *un*soundness of my argument. If you
succeed, then I will say Amen to the Free Trade
formula: 'If a foreign country can supply us with a
commodity cheaper than we ourselves can make it,
better buy it of them.' At the present time, I hold
that Free Trade represents only the interests of the
consumer, and that a national policy implies reserving
a preferential market for its own productions, and so
includes the interests of both the consumer and producer. A wise protective policy regards the interests
of all the industrial classes of the country."

"Mr. Editor" did not reply to this communication,
and so the author of this volume remains an "Un-
teachable Protectionist."

Glasgow Free Trade has certainly provided an
object lesson. The "City Fathers" permitted a loss
to Glasgow labour and capital, and a loss to local
rates and taxes. The "lesson," of course, holds
good with regard to productions of glass, paper,
leather, woollen and other goods, which are capable
of being made in Great Britain and Ireland.

One may quote from "Statistical Abstracts," and
the evidence taken by the Royal Commission on the
Depression of Trade, to prove the destruction of
home industries, but it is all "pooh-poohed," or met
with "no, no," by the average Free Trader.

The fact is, the advocates of the system leave their
case in the hands of certain politico-economic "high
priests," holding briefs for the Cobden Club, and
think it quite sufficient to repeat the usual platitudes.
They do not read the evidence, and what is more,
they do not want to.

We have learned professors scaling the heavens in imagination to give us the aerial food of abstract principles and theories ; they will not come down to the matter-of-fact question of industrial employment for the people, and how our industrial interests can be preserved in a sound state.

A few years ago an eminent professor came to Manchester, and in an address said :—" Home trade is not to be compared in economic advantage with international trade." We may well ask what has become of the old doctrine propounded by Adam Smith :—" The annual labour of every country is the fund which originally supplies it with all the necessities and conveniences of life which it annually consumes ? "

Is there no truth in the value attached to the displacement of capital in the same community, increasing the mass of industrial wealth in that community? The old economists taught that *internal* trade was of paramount importance, and that foreign trade represented the overflow of home production. The professor referred to has estimated the annual gross income of the population of the United Kingdom at £1,200,000,000, and if we allow for interest on investments abroad, etc., we get £1,100,000,000 as the value of the home market ; therefore, we see that home production for home consumption is about five times the value of home production for export.

The professor's address was entirely in the interests of consumers—a class—as if production did not precede consumption.

It is a startling fact that in the years between 1876-

1885, the United Kingdom imported £1,165,000,000 more in merchandise than it exported,[1] and that, during the same period, the United States of America exported £305,000,000 more than they imported. If there is anything in the balance of trade the inference is that during the ten years the United Kingdom became vastly poorer, and the United States of America rapidly increased in wealth. Figure men gloat over foreign trade, but if our consumers are to be supplied by foreign producers, how are our producers to live? Many of our workers do not live, they simply struggle for an existence; our economic slaves of to-day are in some respects worse off than the chattel slaves Samuel Wilberforce worked so hard for, for the latter were generally well-fed and well-housed. A great deal is said to-day upon the parable of labour—the wants of those who live by the labour of their hands; but depend upon it, the state of things to-day is nothing to the state of industrial warfare which will come by-and-by, for we have yet to learn, as a nation, and probably it will be through much suffering, that home trade is of more value than foreign trade. We have yet to learn that true political economy which has for its object the production and equitable distribution of national wealth.

[1] See Chapter VIII., "The Excess of Imports over Exports, and How Paid for."

CHAPTER V.

INDIVIDUALISM *v.* COLLECTIVISM.

OUR PRESENT INDUSTRIAL SYSTEM BREAKING DOWN.

Materialists and Individualists—Political Anarchists—The Impending Deluge—"Anarchy plus the Policeman"—Society can Never be Based Permanently and Successfully on Selfishness—The Free Trade Automatic Machine Smashed Up—Fixed Capital Plundered—Internecine War—Educated Back to a Protective Policy on a Grand and Comprehensive Scale—Changed Attitude of Political Economists of the Manchester School—Free Trade as a Policy ; Individualism as a Theory ; "Leave Alone" as a Maxim of State Condemned, Repudiated, and Cast to the Four Winds of Heaven —A Policy, Social and not Individual, Constructive and not Destructive — Manchester Chamber of Commerce, *Monthly Record* Article—John Bull and Company as a Great Firm, with Branches Abroad in the Shape of vast Colonies and Dependencies.

IN the confusion of thought which prevails in most minds upon public questions, it is not so apparent as it ought to be that during the past fifty or sixty years we have been becoming materialists and individualists, and that our social condition to-day is the result of the experiments and advances which have been made in this direction.

Just as we have political Anarchists among us to-day propounding the monstrous doctrine of the abolition of all law and government as the fulfilment of the idea of liberty and emancipation, so we have had a school of economists who have laid down the same principle as applicable to trade and occupation, and the relations of the State to property and the business of the nation. The interferences of law and of government in this domain, so as to secure stability and honesty, and to regulate and conserve resources and activities with due reference to posterity, so that expansion in these might have proper relation to expansion of population, has been persistently denounced, and, in place of the ideas of the old order of things, there has been put forward the theory of supply and demand, and the natural action and free operation of individual judgment and effort in all matters of occupation, production, and exchange.

Carlyle early in this era perceived and exposed the drift of the impending deluge when he described it as a state of anarchy plus the policeman; and Ruskin, in endeavouring to place art and religion into an ark of safety, unconsciously became the inspiring exponent of the democratic socialism which has risen of late as a counteractive to the materialism and individualism of the age.

The attempt to make everything fit with the formula of the Manchester School has been a conspicuous failure, not only on account of the prophetic resistance of Carlyle and Ruskin, but because also of the inherent impossibility and utter inhumanity of the system.

A priori, it might have been conceded and concluded that society can never be based permanently and successfully on selfishness, either of classes or of individuals, and that it is always true that life is more than meat—even cheap loaves—and the body is more than raiment—even cheap and unlimited shoddy. Accordingly, while Bright and Cobden and their coadjutors were dreaming of an automatic and mechanical freedom, in which constructive and conservative legislation was to become extinct, and nationality was to become obsolete, and all that governments had to do with trade was to leave it alone, Lord Shaftesbury and others busied themselves with Factory and Adulteration Acts ; sanitarians promoted great schemes of public health, involving river purification and buildings supervision ; consumers discovered a new revelation in distributive co-operation, and skilled and unskilled labourers combined in Trade Unions to operate on their own behalf upon the automatic machine of supply and demand.

Competition and Free Trade, therefore, were very early checked in their mad career and confined to specific channels, where the volume of the new force very quickly produced, in these circumstances, a new education for its votaries, and cut out new work for the legislature.

Coffin ships and the sweating system satisfied our seamen and working population *laissez-faire*, and Free Trade was not an unmitigated blessing and divine revelation. " Jerry " buildings and poisoned food and drink products added on another lesson. The investment and re-investment of the surplus capital of the rich classes abroad, and the exploitation of new areas of production thereby, as part and result of our free import policy, in conjunction with intensi-

fied and accelerated competition and economic slavery
at home, exhibited very speedily, in glutted markets
and depreciated prices, the new problems of congestion which have been expressed in the Irish question,
the eight hours labour movement, the coal, dock, and
cotton strikes, the antagonisms of labour and capital,
the reconstruction and writing down of capital in industrial concerns,and the demands upon the legislature,
instead of leaving everything alone, to interfere with
everything.   In fact, we are to have more legislatures
—two instead of one, and three instead of two, and so
on *ad infinitum*, and every one of these legislatures is
to engage its energies in smashing up the automatic
machine in its special locality, and is to provide work
and wages, and free this, that, and the other thing to
the impoverished and maddened proletariat.

Where has our individualism gone to, and how has
it affected our industrial system ?

It has broken itself and our system down, and con-
jured up and confronted us with a confused mass of
appeals to a confused collectivism.

A very brief consideration of the situation will
make manifest how utterly incompatible this re-action
is with the theory of international trade and universal
competition, and that a deadlock is already upon us
in this respect.

If the political unity of our empire and kingdom is
to be broken up by a system of devolution and local
self-government, how will we stand as a community
against the centralising, and unification, and increasing protectionism of foreign States whose competition
in trade we have challenged at home and abroad ?

If all fixed capital has to be plundered, and property and industry are to be harassed by petty and
local interferences, how will competition in its continuance affect our own national areas, and how will
our great industries of production and distribution
compete successfully with those of foreign States in
our own and in foreign markets?

If our employers and landlords are to be so worried
that their profits are cut down to vanishing point and
their capitals to be diminished, while we invite and
continue the unrestricted competition of the foreigner,
how are our mills to be kept going? how is our shipping to remain under the flag? how is cultivation of
the surface of our soil, or the winning of minerals from
its depths, to be carried on?

These are questions which demand consideration,
and must be answered.

The classes without any monetary or proprietary
stake in this country may not seem to care at present
in the internecine war which is going on, but they will
soon be compelled to care when capital abandons the
country, and leaves the soil derelict, and the mills and
the mines idle, and when even foreign investment
ends in collapse and repudiation, as it is bound to do
if all this continues. For true it is, for all time and in
all circumstances, that a nation, whether it consumes
its own productions, or with them purchases commodities from abroad, has no more purchasing power or
means to spend than is derivable from its production
from year to year, and the safe reproduction of its
savings in new forms of investment.   This, therefore,
implies and necessitates conservation and regulation

of industry and resources by a policy of wise protection and imperial solidarity instead of either the
laissez-faire automatic machine folly, or the suicidal
interferences of local and municipal socialisms.

We are being educated back to a protective policy
on a grand and comprehensive scale by the petty and
impossible protectionisms which are growing up out of
the *reductio ad absurdum* of our individualism and our
Free Trade folly.   Accordingly, even the Manchester
School of political economists are changing their
voices and their attitudes, and demanding forms of
Protection for their peculiar and special interests,
which condemn their theories of supply and demand,
and their pet policy of "leave alone."

When India imposes fiscal duties upon imports,
Manchester cotton goods are to be exempted, and
Lancashire thereby to be protected.

The over-production and the natural (low) price of
silver is to be artificially counteracted by a fixed legal
ratio to gold being conferred upon silver as a legal
tender, and the legislatures of the world, along with
our own, instead of leaving silver alone, as everything
was to be left, to the automatic machine, are to interfere to rehabilitate the depreciated value of an over-
produced commodity in relation to the standard, and
to protect Manchester against the competition of
Bombay and the fluctuations (under the automatic
machine) of the rate of exchange.

In doing this (if ever they do it) they will also protect, doubtless, the silver producers abroad, and the
speculators in silver mining shares.

Free Trade as a policy, individualism as a theory,

"leave alone" as a maxim of State, are condemned,
repudiated, cast to the four winds of heaven, and the
political economy of Liberalism and the Manchester
School, relegated to Jupiter and Saturn in this quite
as much as already and by the same party they have
been in the questions of land and labour, by the Irish
policy, and by the industrial legislation which is part
and parcel of the "Newcastle programme."

The existence of the nation, and the welfare of our
industrial community, demand a policy, social and
not individual, constructive and not destructive, conservative and not liberal—as Liberalism has been
understood—and imperial and protective in its prevailing characteristics, instead of parochial and competitive; and this is being demonstrated by the evils
which exist, and the utter inability of the system
which has produced them to provide any remedy
consistent with itself.

In a recent (November, 1893) very able but incon-
clusive article in the *Monthly Record* of the Manchester
Chamber of Commerce, dealing with the problem of
the minimum or living wage demand, the writer made
one or two very interesting admissions, which have a
strong bearing upon the subject of the present
chapter.

Among other things it was there said—in a quotation from a letter by Sir William Houldsworth, Bart.
—that it was possible with advantage to combine the
active principles both of co-operation and of competition. This was, in effect, admitting and enforcing
the doctrine that economic truth rested between those
antagonistic extremes, and that the one might be use-

fully modified by the other.   It is late in the day for
this school to make such an interesting discovery, and
it is far from my purpose in these remarks to deal
slightingly with such an important statement.   But
what is it, after all, but recognising in a somewhat
sullen and ingenious way the manifest failure and
fallacy of the gospel of cheapness and the evangel of
universal competition?   The admission was made in
connection with the no less interesting statement,
which has hitherto only been made by Protectionists,
that high wages and high efficiency of production,
and also increased purchasing power and increased
consumption, could also go together.   This, at the
very least, qualifies the doctrines of cheapness and of
competition in a most important manner, and dis-
credits the foundations upon which the Free Trade
policy of this country has been built up.

The desired cheapness is not to be cheapness at
any price, and Free Trade and competition are not
to be Free Trade and competition in the unalloyed
and unmitigated acceptation in which they were
originally propounded.

But how far beyond mere platitudes can the
Manchester party, without conversion, go in the
working out of any practical reconciliation of co-
operation and competition?   Can they succeed in
any partial application of the combination, and maintain our present anomalous fiscal policy?   Can they
reconcile universal competition in our markets with any
associative efforts which shall secure higher remuneration—say to our farmers, and higher wages to our
rural labourers and skilled and unskilled artizans,

whom they have ground under the Juggernaut wheels of universal and unreciprocated foreign competition ? Can they reconcile their cosmopolitan and competitive policy with the association of John Bull and Company as a great firm with branches abroad in the shape of vast colonies and dependencies ?

Will they allow to British citizenship and to trade under the flag in every quarter of British world-wide dominion, the enjoyment of an effective preference over foreigners, and to combine competition with association, and modify Free Trade and its absurd corollaries by patriotism and common sense? Only if they are prepared to be converted in this fashion, can they enter into the Kingdom of Heaven which they desiderate in such empty platitudes, and realise the workable application of the benevolent admission, and the delightful discovery they have made : because anything short of this would most certainly nullify any partial application of the combination which might otherwise be attempted.

CHAPTER VI.

NATIONAL EFFACEMENT, OR AN IMPERIAL POLICY: WHICH IS IT TO BE?

The Critical Point, a Choice must be made Affecting the Existence of our Nation and Empire—We will Never, Now, be the Workshop of the World—The British Workman Robbed of his Markets—Lord Salisbury Exempting Land from its Special Burdens; the Wiltshire Proposal—A Nice Piece of Wiltshire Bacon—Nearing the Rapids, are we to "Shoot Niagara," a Spectacle and a Warning for History and Humanity?—Political Salvation.

THE British people are being driven by force of circumstances to a critical point, where the choice must be finally and decisively made of abiding the last consequences of the Free Trade policy or of escaping them, in the only possible way, before it is too late to escape.

It is no mere academic choice, but one supremely practical, involving tremendous consequences to humanity and to civilisation, which will have to be made.

It involves the continued existence of our nation and empire.

Let it be remembered seriously, that Great Britain is not, and never now can be, the workshop of the world.

This dream, which was the original justification of

74

our Free Trade policy, is over. Upon what production and exchanges, therefore, can British capital and labour expect to be employed to provide continued and sufficient reproduction for the one and employment for the other, so as to continue national life into future years and centuries?

Capital, unless stimulated by profit, and encouraged by security to alliance with industry, languishes and diminishes, and takes to itself wings and flies away.

The joint efforts of labour and capital create results which are only realisable into national wealth if there are adequate markets for the exchange of the surplusses of production over consumption. If there are no such adequate markets, these efforts are paralysed by congestion, and waste and poverty, in place of wealth and riches, are the results.

Let us suppose, then, for a moment, that Great Britain does not choose to protect, by an Imperial policy, her own markets for her own labour and capital.

Population will continue to grow much as it has done. How is that population to be provided for, if Protectionist countries continue their Protection against us, deny us fair exchange, and are allowed to deluge and capture our markets with their surplusses in production, as they have of late been doing?

Let it be repeated, we will never now be the workshop of the world. Foreign nations will never adopt Free Trade.

Protection has succeeded in solving or assisting their fiscal problems, and, at the same time, in making them industrially independent of us. It has done

more ; it has enabled them not only to possess
and control their home markets, but to capture
the external markets upon which our hopes de-
pended.

What have we left ?   India and our various
colonies and dependencies.   Of what certain value in
these circumstances are the various extensions of the
empire to each other, or to the mother country, under
the policy of commercial treaties on the Free Trade—
at all costs—basis, and the most favoured nation
clause ?   The time has come when these treaties
must be denounced, the shackles imposed by them
upon our colonies and dependencies must be burst,
and the fiscal freedom and unity of our empire must
be restored, or we shall lose that empire.

That is what is in store for us as the last and
certain penalty of Free Trade folly.   What about
Africa ?   The starving steed of British industry and
commerce cannot wait for the grass to grow in that
quarter.   It will be a long time, indeed, supposing
we secured Africa to ourselves against foreign competition, for the naked barbarians of Africa to become customers for our highly finished manufactures.
What about China and Japan ?

Our Free Trade folly has created competing production for these markets in quarters of the world
which are geographically and economically fitted to
overwhelm our efforts to retain them for the United
Kingdom.   This is well known.   The British capital
invested in Indian mills, Russian mills, United States
mills ;—and why not also in Chinese and Japanese
mills some day ?—all this is robbing, and will rob,

the British workman of these markets, as a source of profit and an outlet for surplus manufactures.

"Oh, but," say the Free Traders of one set, "we will settle the silver question in our favour by bi-metallism, and transfer trade advantages in the East to ourselves." Well, this would be another and less justifiable form of Protection than a commercial union of the empire would be.

Another set like Lord Salisbury say, "Oh, but, as we cannot depart from Free Trade, we must get the labour of the people and the capital of our rich classes back to the land by exempting land from its special burdens." Precisely; but would not this also be Protection, and Protection at the wrong end?

What would these politicians say to this, who believe and declare that land should bear every burden —that the whole weight of taxation should fall upon land?

It is the purpose of those politicians to tax the present proprietors of land out of their possessions in land in this country. Will not any movement, therefore, to relieve and secure these landlords by exempting their property from taxation be regarded and denounced as a piece of class protection? So it seems. All efforts to evade the protection of the empire upon a grand and a wise scale involve some plan of foolish protection of a class upon a petty scale. Why not, therefore, *protect the empire?* and, by protecting the great whole, protect unquestionably all that is included in the whole?

Before Lord Salisbury's Wiltshire proposal is likely to be seriously entertained, a large number of industrial pursuits and investments will be in quite as bad a plight as agriculture, from foreign competition and unremunerative prices. When all these are equally pauperised by Free Trade, shall they also be relieved from taxation for the sake of sticking to the bitter end to the mistaken policy of Free Trade?

Free Trade is such a nice piece of Wiltshire bacon, it seems, that we must needs burn our whole house down for the sake of roasting it!

No, no, it won't do. Nothing will avail; and there is no escape from national effacement, if we drift on in our present policy.

We are nearing the rapids. Are we to " shoot Niagara," a spectacle and a warning for history and humanity? Or are we to lay hold of protection of the empire and political salvation to arise to a great opportunity, and clothe ourselves with imperial grandeur, and take to ourselves the Imperial power, which is possible, and *reign?*

CHAPTER VII.

IN the introductory chapter, it is stated in regard to
the Anti-Corn Law agitation that the whole history
of that movement had been falsified by the Free
Traders.

This charge will now be repeated and examined, and a short review of the actual circumstances of the country at that period will be made.

It has been represented broadly that the Corn Laws were an unjustifiable protection of the landlord interest to the detriment of the manufacturing interests of the nation ; that these laws made bread artificially dear and employment scarce and unprofitable, and that their abolition ushered in an era of plenty and expansion, and produced in the sequel " leaps and bounds " of national prosperity. It is not difficult to-day, after the political strife and tumult which accompanied and incited that great controversy have given place to other and different contentions, to expose the abounding misrepresentations which have had such abiding force, and to rescue the truth of the matter, and place it clearly and unquestionably before the reader.

It is quite possible also that, at the time, the real circumstances and needs of the country were not properly understood in the clamour of the times, and amid the passions which were engendered out of party strife and the conflict of class interests.

We know now, at all events, that the "leaps and bounds " of national prosperity have passed away, that the great manufacturing and commercial interests, which rose upon the ruins of our agricultural greatness, have got into trouble and distress, and that we still have Free Trade in the form of free or un-taxed imports of foreign competing production.

Some evident mistake and fallacy, therefore, exists in the Free Trade argument, and some great errors obviously are incorporated in the history of our times according to the Free Trade school.

We know, further, that we have not converted the world to Free Trade.

In the clear perspective of historical retrospect, and with a higher vantage ground, aided by the tests of experience, we will be enabled to understand these circumstances better than has hitherto been possible.

To understand the needs of the country at the time, which determined the policy which the circumstances demanded, there are three distinct subjects— matters of fact—which require to be investigated. The first relates to the Corn Laws themselves ; the second, to the then necessities of trade and commerce ; and the third, to the problems of taxation and statesmanship in connection with the political party platforms and popular feelings of the time.

It is in an unprejudiced and clear view of facts in regard to these three subjects that the true history can alone be understood and expressed.

The Corn Laws, or the fiscal and parliamentary control of the exports of British and the import of foreign corn, were essentially the provision of statesmanship for the protection of the nation in the matter of food supplies and the cultivation of the soil. The policy of exercising this control was originally adopted to regulate, and even prohibit, the exportation of home-grown food products when the home demand pulled upon the supply. The people generally, and especially those of the towns, were for ages protected against foreign demand and mercantile disposal of the corn of the country in periods of scarcity.

F

In these circumstances, the Sovereigns and Parliaments of England taxed the exports of English corn with due reference to the claims and necessities of the English people. This was while England produced corn and food supplies generally largely in excess of the wants of the population.[1] As population increased to a par with the then productive capacity of the soil, of course the export of grain ceased to be a question, because no foreign market was at all likely to offer any inducement to exportation ; but, the providing a sufficient food supply for an increased and increasing population without becoming dependent upon foreign supplies, which might be interrupted in time of war, became the great and urgent question of patriotism and public policy.

After the union of Scotland with England, when the United Kingdom, including Ireland, finally became in a sense one Commonwealth, political econo-

---

[1] Amount of the Total Sum Paid in Bounty upon the Exportation of Grain.

Years.					Amount paid.
1697 to 1774*	...	...	...	...	£6,237,176
1775 to 1795	...	...	...	...	786,426
1796 to 1805	...	...	...	...	21,752
1807	...	...	...	...	78
					£7,045,432

* From 1697 to 1774 our total excess of exports were 30,968,366 quarters of grain. In 1790 our imports began to exceed exports.

Amount of the Total Sum Paid in Bounty upon the Importation of Grain.

Years.					Amount paid.
1796 to 1805	...	...	...	...	£2,853,537
1807	...	...	...	...	129
1810	...	...	...	...	138
					£2,853,804

mists directed public opinion and legislative effort to
increasing the cultivatable area by the encouragement
of improvements and the inclusion of inferior soils
into the amount of land under tillage.

Treatises were written, surveys were carried through,
reports were submitted to Parliament, and strenuous
and successful efforts were made to raise the productive capacity of the country to a secure and hopeful
proportion to the necessities of the population. Poets
and statesmen alike encouraged yeoman enterprise
and invoked public blessings upon the policy of re-
covering and reclaiming waste places, and making
wildernesses rejoice, and upon the effort which should
make two blades of grass or corn grow where only
one had grown before, and which replaced heath and
herbage by fruitful crops. Capital and labour were
thus attracted to and retained upon the soil over the
length and breadth of the land, and the continuance
of the system was secured by the imposition of duties
upon importation levied with a view to preventing the
less fertile portions from going out of cultivation
through the returns becoming unprofitable. For a
long time general satisfaction followed this policy, and
no word of trouble was heard. Food was abundant
and cheap, and the country safe and prosperous, and
Great Britain rapidly rose to prominence, and even
supremacy in Europe. Then, on account of the very
plenteousness and cheapness of food, in conjunction
with war taxes upon the land, as upon other taxable
subjects, agricultural distress set in, expressing itself
in demands for such increased duties as would maintain profitable production in the least profitable areas,

and maintain a bottom or minimum price for wheat—variable of course from time to time.

The fact of agricultural distress which appears and re-appears during the existence of the Corn Laws, and which was the occasion of so many proposals in the country and in Parliament during that period for the relief of agriculture, is quite inconsistent with the assertion that the Corn Laws produced dear prices. The Corn Laws did for the greater part of their existence what they were intended to do—that is, to maintain an extensive cultivation of British corn, and the very extent of that production and consequent competition resulted in prices so low as to be regarded as being ruinous to the agricultural interests in the less favoured districts of wheat production.

If again, we take the actual prices of wheat ruling since the end of the last century, we will find no evidence to the contrary of this, but very interesting and decisive evidence that high prices, when they occurred, resulted from causes altogether outside of the duties, and that low prices were in no wise the result of our importation.

To understand the situation properly, we must divide the period under review into three. We have first (beginning, of course, only at the end of the century) the period when a low or nominal duty of sixpence per quarter upon imported wheat was in operation, with higher duties only permitted after the price fell below a given point, and increasing in amount in a given proportion to the continued fall in price. This covers from 1790 to 1815; it was a period during which, although Corn Laws were in existence conferring power to impose high duties and even to prohibit importation, they were not operative upon prices or supply, for the simple reason that the price (due to the domestic supply) was for the most part so low as to keep down importation. It was practically a period of free imports, but without any import to speak of.[1] There was no imposition of any duty heavier than 6d., for the most part, because when the price was high—which it sometimes was through scarcity—there was no duty beyond the 6d., and when the prices were low, which was often the case, there was no importation.

According to a chart which was published in October, 1885, in the *Fair Trade Journal*, and which is strictly accurate and in keeping with the statistics of the period, the price of wheat between 1795 and 1799 ranged from 54s. per quarter to 78s., at which prices there was no great amount of importation.

The duty of 6d. per quarter was then paid when wheat was 54s. and over, and was only at 2s. 6d. per quarter should the price fall below 54s. and not below 50s. After it should get below 50s. (by the Act of 1791) the duty was to be 24s. 3d., but with a bounty on exportation at 46s. per quarter.

This was to provide that 46s. per quarter should be a bottom price for wheat, as the lowest possible at which cultivation of the inferior soils could be maintained. But as the natural price of wheat during

---

[1] Amount of the Total Sum paid upon the Importation ot Grain.

Years.				Duty raised.
1660 to 1795	...	...	...	nil.
1796 to 1812	...	...	...	£488,184 3 2¼
1813	...	...	...	Records destroyed by fire.

this period was always above 50s., no duty higher than 2s. 6d. per quarter was practically exigible from 1790 to 1815. For the most part the duty was only 6d., on account of the natural price of wheat being at and above the 54s.

The price jumped up to the abnormally high figures of 120s. and 127s. respectively in 1801 and 1812, but this was owing entirely to scarcity from deficient harvests, and the *state of war* in which this country was engaged on the Continent and elsewhere, and the bloody wars of the continental nations. It was not due to the operation of heavy duties upon imports of foreign wheat seeking admission into the country, but was part and parcel of the calamities of the Napoleonic wars.

The next period of natural division is between 1815 and 1846, when the Corn Law system was abolished. The price of wheat was as low as 39s. 4d. a quarter in 1835; it was 44s. 7d. in 1822, and it only jumped up on one occasion, in 1817, to 96s. 11d., falling rapidly in each succeeding harvest to 44s. 7d. in 1822, then gradually up and down, and up again and down again, during the next sixteen years, from 70s. 6d. (the highest during these years) in 1839, to 39s. 4d. in 1835, according to supply and demand, but averaging over the whole of these thirty odd years 58s. 6d. per quarter.

[1] The Repeal of the Corn Laws, which followed

[1] 1814 to 1846.	Quarters imported.	Total £	Avg. duty per qr. s. d.
Wheat and wheat flour	29,224,790	8,613,587	5 $10\frac{5}{8}$
Barley and barley meal	6,925,403	1,265,200	3 8
Oats and oatmeal	12,312,302	1,920,566	3 $2\frac{3}{8}$

£11,799,353

1846, did not very materially affect prices, and there were dearer prices a long way during some years of free imports than the average during the Corn Laws. In 1855 the price of wheat rose to 75s. per quarter; in 1867 it was touching 65s., and during the first thirty years of free imports the average price of wheat was 52s. 1d. per quarter against 58s. 6d. of an average during the last thirty years of the Corn Laws. *What brought prices down was not the repeal or absence of Corn Laws, but the increased production abroad, and the extension of railways from producing areas abroad to the sea-boards, coupled with the contemporaneous development of ocean transport by steam vessels.* The opening of the Suez Canal also, by shortening the route to India and bringing Indian production into competition (1884-5) with American in our markets, brought down the price of American wheat, and procured low prices for wheat in every market of the world.

It is nothing less than a historical and commercial as well as a political, falsehood of the first magnitude to ascribe the economic results of steam transport to the abolition of the Corn Laws. Corn Laws might, could, and should have been continued with every advantage to our tax-payers and consumers—varying, of course, with the exigencies of the times—all along.

The objectionable accidents of their operation during the "sliding scale" of duties : that is, the gambling by speculators ("Forestallers "),[1] on the rise

---

[1] These speculative dealers in bread stuffs—in the days of slow and difficult transit, and isolation of localities—cornered

or fall of the duties, would have been effectually removed, beyond any question, not only by legislation,
if that had been necessary, but by the sub-marine
cable, and by the steam transport service.

The Repeal of the Corn Laws was in reality *a
blind and mad Act of high Protection to the foreigner
and the capitalists interested in foreign investment
and a foreign corn trade with this country.* It was
also an indirect protection (for a time only) of our
manufacturing classes, by bringing about the collapse
of agriculture in the areas which were less fertile, and
confining agricultural production and competition in
Great Britain to a restricted area, because it drove
population from agricultural pursuits into seeking
refuge in the towns, *and so cheapened the value of
labour to the manufacturing classes.*

It withdrew capital also from agriculture to commerce, and to urban industries, and so effected an
industrial and economic revolution.   Had there still
been Corn Laws continued, and all the land under
wheat maintained in that production, the supply of
our markets from home production and from abroad
would have kept the price of wheat down to the
lowest price at which the land of this country at all
suitable for wheat could have continued to grow it.
The purchaser or seller at a lower price abroad would
have had to pay to the British Exchequer the difference—less commissions and costs of freights—in the

corn, and made temporary and local scarcity, and a good deal
of distress.   The "Forestallers" were "Free Traders," and
Protection got the blame of the suffering created by their
crimes.

shape of duty. Taxes of an internal nature could have been reduced to the relief of industry, and *the means of bargain would have been retained in our fiscal system, for securing advantageous openings abroad for our surplus manufactures, and realising trade exchanges adequate to our growing commerce and manufacturing development.*

To substantiate this theoretical statement, we have only to inquire what have been the experiences of continental countries, who have maintained their protective systems and their Corn Laws all along, and who have enjoyed every advantage due to the world's increased production, and the modern facilities of communication and transport.

France and Germany have preserved their agriculture, and increased their agricultural area and production year by year (as well as vastly expanding their manufactures), while *our soil has been going out of cultivation,* and *Irish prosperity has been so grievously reduced.* And both France and Germany have had quite as cheap, and even cheaper, wheat than we have had. They have had the advantage of the duties plus the supply, both domestic and foreign, and these duties have been a deduction from the otherwise possible profit of the exporters thence.

Tables of German and French Prices Compared with British Prices.[1]

Wheat, per cwt.—(shillings).

	1883.	1884.	1885.	1886.	1887.	1888.	1889.	1890.
Germany,	9·40	8·17	8·17	7·61	8·28	8·61	9·39	9·77
United Kingdom,	9·81	8·41	7·83	7·55	7·65	7·68	7·69	7·89

[1] There is a general notion that, if the price of wheat in the United Kingdom is, say, 28s. per quarter, it must be 36s. 9d. in

Wheat, per ton.

	England.			France.			Germany.		
1872	£14	5	0	£13	10	0	£11	11	0
1873	14	14	0	14	12	0	11	17	0
1874	14	9	0	14	7	0			
1875	11	5	0	11	2	0	No returns.		
1876	11	11	0	12	3	0	9	12	0
1877	14	4	0	13	13	0	No returns.		
1878	11	12	0	13	9	0	10	10	0
1879	11	0	0	12	15	0	9	19	0
1880	11	2	0	13	7	0	No returns.		
1881	11	7	0	12	18	0	10	3	0
1882	11	5	0	12	11	0	No returns.		
1883	10	8	0	11	4	0	8	13	0

France, because of the French import duty of 8s. 9d., *i.e.* our price plus the duty. But supply and demand regulates prices, and the incidence of import taxation turns upon the amount of internal production to satisfy home requirements. The production of wheat and rye-wheat in France (1880-1890) was enormous, and wheat sent into that country would have to be invoiced, plus the duty, to compete with prices ruling there. It does not follow that the price here will prevail in France. Our market may be glutted, and then exporters would have to sell in another market.

In proof of this contention, I refer the reader to a table given in the appendix to the Third Report of the Royal Commission appointed to inquire into the Depression of Trade and Industry, which shows that in France wheat was, on an average, just 2s. 6d. a quarter cheaper than it was in England, with the United Kingdom Corn Laws abolished from 1846 down to 1870 ; that wheat has, moreover, been, on an average, *cheaper in France than in England during the whole period* (1846-1883) ; and the same table shows that, while the average price of wheat in England for the four years preceding the abolition of the Corn Laws was only £2 12s. 4½d. per quarter, the average price of wheat from 1846 down to 1875 was £2 12s. 11¾d. per quarter.

The French import duty will have curtailed the middleman's profits somewhat, and caused the foreign exporter to pay "a market toll." At any rate, the duties on wheat, and the higher

I now come to the second consideration proposed in this chapter, namely, the demands or
exigencies of our manufacturing interests at that
period. Let it be borne in mind that Arkwright was
perfecting his great mechanical improvements in
cotton spinning machinery in 1765 or thereabout.
We may easily allow our minds to revert to that
period as the one which ushered in those wonderful
developments of time and labour-saving implements
which conferred upon Great Britain immensely accelerated and increased means of production and
distribution in relation to the labour and capital employed, and in relation to the powers of her competitors abroad. Great Britain was bringing to birth
those phenomenal energies and resources associated
with steam and electricity, and the names of Watt
and Stephenson, of Fulton and Bell, and of Farraday
in later years.

If the reader, however, has attentively read the
preceding portion of this chapter, he will more clearly
understand the great motive which was inciting the
inventive faculties of Englishmen and Scotchmen to
increase production, in relation to labour and capital
employed, by labour-saving appliances in every
direction and detail of industrial effort. Labour was
or had been scarce and dear, because population had
been occupied to such an extent upon the soil, or
engaged in wars upon land and sea.

Capital also had been largely interested in an
extended agricultural system, causing dear money to

duties on flour, have not been oppressive, *owing to the volume
of internal production.*

manufacturers, and war-taxes and risks added heavy
burdens to industry, at the expense of profits.

It is said that cart-loads of children were conveyed
from distant districts, from the poorhouses and such
like, to the rising centres of manufacturing enterprise,
and this very simple statement of a matter of fact,
along with certain other statements in the literature
of the day, such as Mrs. Opie's appeals on behalf of
the oppressed children, irresistibly prove and explain
the economic tendencies of our manufacturing classes.

The rapid introduction of machinery without compensating or humane provision for displaced labour,
and before new markets for increased production
could be opened up, entailed unspeakable and wide-
spread local distresses and abounding poverty and
pauperism among victimised communities in the
days of slow posts and stage coaches, and before
society had developed the provident and philan-
thropic organisations of later years.

All this misery was *falsely ascribed to the Corn
Laws,* on the pretence and alleged ground that these
Laws protected the aristocracy and the interests of
agriculture at the expense of the proletariat of the
towns.

The truth was, that the middle classes of the
towns—the bourgeoisie class—were agitating for
political power and aggrandisement, and they seized
upon the misery, due to economic causes, for purposes of political capital to themselves, and to mis-
direct the resentment and hatred of the lower orders
on to the country aristocracy, instead of towards
themselves.

The great combinations of English labour took their origin in these circumstances, inspired by a spirit derived from the French Revolution, and threatened in secret societies a social upheaval in demanding the rights of ,life as superior to those of property in those days of the displacement of their labour by machinery.

Writers like the late Charles Knight undertook the task of educating them in the knowledge of their ultimate interest in the increased demand which would eventually follow the substitution of mechanical for manual labour ; but the desperate and immediate miseries of their situation threatened to culminate in a Chartist Revolution. The middle classes adroitly captured the forces of disorder as a means to their attaining the preponderating political power which they determined on, and so they deliberately falsified the situation by becoming the pretended champions of the people against the aristocracy. Everything was laid to the Corn Laws. The country party was selected as the national scape-goat upon which the sins of the nation were to be laid, and a new issue was raised out of the situation which was contrived entirely in the supposed interest of the towns, and for the humiliation of the landed interests.

There was one element of extreme plausibility in the policy and argument of the manufacturers which must have had considerable weight, although it was entirely optimistic. It was the expectation and conclusion that the markets of the Continent would be opened on a wider scale to British manufactures, especially cotton goods, if the Corn Laws were abolished.

Great Britain was the dearest and most profitable market to which wheat from the Danubian and Baltic and other foreign provinces could be exported. The fallacious doctrine or statement that corn or other duties upon competing imports were taxes upon consumers was unconsciously contradicted by the inconsistent admission of the advantages which would be conferred upon foreign countries by the opening of our ports free to their exports ; and it was expected and predicted, that for the sake of these great advantages to their agriculture, foreign governments would admit British manufactures more and more freely into their markets, and afford to Great Britain the much desiderated monopoly of being the workshop of the world.

But no such cosmopolitan division of labour was entertained by continental countries, who, instead of advancing in the direction of Free Trade, advanced in the contrary direction of more effective Protection.

They could not abandon their manufacturing interests to annihilation under our superior competition, or contemplate a merely servile and agrarian basis for their civilisation. But it was thought by many people at the time that Cobden and Bright were inspired prophets in predicting that this would happen, and the wish which, in this case, was father to the thought, easily induced a belief in this sanguine anticipation.

We have seen that the abolition of the duties, alongside of the advantage to foreign States of our free market—which doubtless induced them to produce more for our market—*only affected the average price of wheat for thirty years some six shillings or so a quarter.* Whatever expansion did take place in our imports under the new system and with the improved carrying facilities which were afterwards developed, only realised the anticipations of barter to an extent compatible with the continued existence of duties ; *for the foreign nations continued their duties upon what we sold to them whatever the advantage they derived from our free ports.*

Still, Lancashire made Great Britain rely upon certain axioms, such as : " The more we buy from abroad, the more we must sell to the foreigner," since " goods are paid for by goods," and " all trade is barter." These phrases being swallowed without question or investigation, it was fully believed that expansion of manufacturing industry would abundantly compensate for agricultural depression, and that every foreign creditor, through our free import system, would balance the account with British manufacturers.

The investment of British capital abroad to produce for our markets in alliance with foreign land and foreign labour, under our Free Trade policy, has falsified this expectation and given us imports immensely and progressively in excess of our exports.

Our total foreign trade is greater only because science has made greater production and distribution possible, and so the total trade of foreign States, which are Protectionist, is greater also, but with this difference, that Protection preserves to these countries their home markets and home investments and a favourable balance of trade ; whereas, *free imports are attracting and transferring British capital abroad, and giving us a balance of trade altogether fatal to the prosperity of our manufacturing classes.*

The last subject to be very briefly considered is that of the problems of taxation and statesmanship pressing upon the nation at the period of the Corn Law agitation. Up to that period, land and agriculture had been treated as the principal source of national wealth and revenue. Corn Laws were, therefore, naturally regarded as fiscal duties countervailing the direct burdens on land, just as customs duties still countervail the duties of excise.

The rise of trade and manufactures and of the middle class, after the peace, brought into importance a new source of wealth and revenue derivable from profits in trade. The doctrine of buying in the cheapest market made fiscal duties affecting this class a most objectionable source of revenue, because all duties were ignorantly supposed to increase the cost of production to this class. The profits of trade being eked out of competition, every such producer has always been keenly conscious of his interests also as a consumer, and determined to have as free a hand as possible, so as to buy in the cheapest and sell in the dearest market.

There is no doubt that this class sincerely believed that the abolition of all duties upon imports in the ordinary course of trade would give them this advantage. Their idea was that industry should be free from all liability to contribute to the revenue.

Statesmen, therefore, who desired to conciliate this class and the masses influenced by these arguments, gave way to the specious sophistries about " freeing industry from burdens," and contemplated such alternative methods of taxation as fitted in with this new shibboleth of fiscal policy. The income tax was to take the place of import duties, and as a means of revenue, as a measure of protection to this class.

To tax property and not to tax industry sounded very well, and made a good political cry with the ignorant and unthinking, who supposed that it was possible to confine the incidence of taxation in this way.

It was powerful enough to lead the nation astray upon the whole question of taxation and finance.

There was another very important factor in the matter of taxation, and that was the Poor Laws. Previous to 1832 there was a very large amount of out-door relief maintained, much in the spirit of the feudal obligation of the proprietors in by-past times, of which it was a survival, to maintain life as well as property. During the depression of agriculture through low prices during the Corn Laws, which has already been adverted to, this system of out-door relief to able-bodied poor became obnoxious to the class of economists who promoted Free Trade doctrines. As a system, it imposed a very heavy burden upon property in congested districts ; but it afforded relief to poverty, and prevented the dispersion of the rural population. In the struggle for existence under competition, all doles and gifts to ameliorate poverty are used to eke out life, and labour surrenders them to capital under supply and demand.

G

The alteration of the Poor Laws in 1832 terminated this assistance out of the rates to agricultural labourers, which was regarded by the middle classes as another bounty on agriculture, and so effected the dispersion of surplus labour into urban pursuits, and increased the competition, and secured a glut of labour in the towns, thereby keeping down wages in a way much more agreeable to the manufacturing class, and more conformable to their ideas of political economy. *The Poor Law Reform of 1832 reveals the drift of the saviours of 1846.*

As has been already stated—in the introductory chapter—Trades Unionism developed on the part of the working classes an antidote of a protective character to this policy. Curiously enough, these unions, both in their provident and their protective aspects, undertook the whole charge of the old Poor Law system for behoof of the able-bodied poor, so far, at least, as their members were concerned. The other great provident working-class organisations, which soon afterwards grew to such huge dimensions, almost completely, in conjunction with Trade Unions, undertook the relief of able-bodied poverty, and transferred the burden, amid a great deal of Pickwickian gratulation, from the shoulders of property to the wages of the working classes. The altered statistics resulting from this adroit strategy and the new Poor Laws was afterwards adduced in Cobden Club leaflets as a convincing proof of the benefits of Free Trade in reducing pauperism !

CHAPTER VIII.

THE EXCESS OF IMPORTS OVER EXPORTS, AND HOW PAID FOR.

Free Traders Gloating over the "Excess"—The "Modest" Figures of 1870-1874 — "Up-to-date" Statistics — The "Barter Theory" Tested—The Present Balance of Trade— A Comparison, 1870-1874 with 1876-1879 — Imports of Agricultural Produce, of the Principal Competing Manufactures, of the Principal Raw Materials, and of Chemicals and Dye-Stuffs—The General Result—The Summit of our Prosperity Reached—The Regretful Answer—"The Greater the Excess of Imports the Wealthier the Nation"—No Relative Expansion in our Foreign Trade, no Elasticity in our Home Trade—The Enormous Increase of Imported Manufactures in 1886—Plain Unvarnished Facts — Our Position as a Nation analogous to a certain Merchant— Imports and Exports of Gold and Silver Bullion and Specie —The "Re-Export" Trade—Spellbound to the Theories of Free Trade — Naked Facts — Investments in Foreign Countries—"Dead Men's Profits and Wages"—Imports should be Paid for by *Live Men's* Earnings—Profits of the Carrying Trade — No Compensation — The Transfer of Securities—Ignorant Delusion—*Reductio ad Absurdum*— Diagrams of International Trading and Accounts.

THERE was a time when Free Traders positively gloated over the excess of imports over exports ; we were told that the larger the excess the greater was the degree of our national prosperity. Well, *if that be so, we should just now be living in very prosperous times.* No ; when the country was doing well, 1870-1874—the "leaps and bounds" period—the excess of

99

imports over exports was represented by very modest figures.

To assume that goods imported are necessarily paid for by goods exported is ridiculous, in the face of official statistics ; there undoubtedly exists an " adverse balance of trade," [1] which must be adjusted in some form or another.   For instance :—

Volume and Balance of Trade.

	Twelve Months Ended	
1894.	August 31.	Dec. 31, 1893.
Imports	£413,610,078	£405,067,690
British exports	215,400,005	218,496,246
Re-exports	56,018,842	58,935,595
	£685,028,925	£682,499,531

	Twelve Months Ended	
1893.	August 31.	Dec. 31, 1892.
Imports	£408,691,846	£423,793,882
British exports	222,660,616	227,077,053
Re-exports	63,993,841	64,563,113
	£695,346,303	£715,434,048

Excess of Imports.		
1894	£142,191,231	£127,635,849
1893	122,037,389	132,153,716

Here, it must be noted, we have a less total trade, and an increasing excess of imports over exports.

Dissecting the exports of British and Irish produce and manufacture for the year ended August 31, 1894, compared with the same period (1893), we get the following :—

[1] See table at the end of this chapter.

	Year.	
	1894.	1893.
Class I.		
Animals	£563,933	£703,899
Class II.		
Food and drink	10,771,102	10,467,245
Class III.		
Raw materials	19,286,786	17,871,547
Class IV.		
(a) Textiles	96,424,702	97,714,049
(b) Metals	27,876,463	32,577,558
(c) Machinery	14,426,554	13,519,972
(d) Apparel	8,973,558	9,691,148
(e) Chemicals	8,370,026	9,065,277
(f) Other articles	27,632,665	30,037,718
(g) Parcel Post	1,074,216	1,012,203
Total value	£215,400,005	£222,660,616
Foreign and colonial exports	56,018,842	63,993,841
Total exports	£271,418,847	£286,654,457

Dissecting the imports from foreign countries and British possessions for the year ended August 31, 1894, compared with the same period (1893), we arrive at the following :—

	Year.	
	1894.	1893.
Class I.		
Animals	£8,479,158	£6,698,639
Class II.—Food :		
(a) Free	143,654,115	144,714,434
(b) Dutiable	24,244,920	25,939,240
Tobacco	3,635,592	3,504,955
Class III.		
Metals	19,868,344	20,115,313
Class IV.		
Chemicals	6,515,647	6,427,259
Class V.		
Oils	7,474,801	7,276,773
Class VI.		
Raw textiles	72,731,491	70,653,505
Class VII.		
Do. other	42,706,362	40,936,385
Class VIII.		
Manufactured articles	66,950,080	66,625,172
Class IX.		
(a) Miscellaneous	16,613,555	15,216,432
(b) Parcel Post	736,013	583,739
Total imports	£413,610,078	£408,691,846

The reader can examine the items of these tables and form his own conclusion as to the state of our foreign trade up to date.

In 1840—seven years before the wonderful Free Trade principle was affirmed—the value of the exports of British produce exceeded that of the imports of foreign produce by £48,000,000 ; therefore, if the barter theory (or the contention that exports are the equivalent of imports) holds good, *it implies that British foreign trade at that period was conducted at an enormous loss by British traders, which conclusion is palpably absurd.*

Looking to the present balance of trade, it is apparent that the excess of imports over exports does *not* consist of raw materials for production or of labour products which we cannot manufacture ourselves ; if otherwise, we should have no difficulty in settling the adverse balance. But it is evident that the excess is made up of food products and manufactures *competing* with our own production. The following statistics bear upon this contention ; I take the prosperous years 1870-1-2-3 and 4, and compare them with the years 1876-7-8 and 9, to arrive at the facts of the case.

The difference between imports and exports (omitting odd figures), 1870, £59 millions ; 1871, £47 millions ; 1872, £40 millions ; 1873, £60 millions ; whilst in 1876-9, years of depression, the difference was—1876, £118 millions; 1877, £142 millions; 1878, £123 millions ; 1879, £114 millions. This clearly establishes the fact that the years when the difference was smallest *were the years when our prosperity was at its zenith.*

I now go a step further and show the reason for this conclusion. In the years 1870-1-2-3 we imported of agricultural produce :—

1870.	1871.	1872.	1873.
£54,962,068	£67,265,341	£77,252,960	£83,225,856

Average, £70,676,556.

Taking the years 1876-7-8-9 we find imports of exactly the same products :—

1876.	1877.	1878.	1879.
£91,742,864	£103,003,530	£102,190,107	£104,510,730

Average, £100,362,007.

Let us now look at our imports of the *principal* manufactures competing against us for the same years. They are thus :—

1870.	1871.	1872.	1873.
£33,695,191	£29,426,958	£32,756,804	£35,063,208

Average, £32,735,540.

1876.	1877.	1878.	1879.
£42,571,292	£45,263,168	£45,195,482	£42,816,640

Average, £43,961,645.

I will now consider our *principal* imports of raw material, to see if there is a corresponding increase under this heading. They are as follows :—

1870.	1871.	1872.	1873.
£137,348,511	£145,853,262	£149,015,210	£154,125,629

Average, £146,585,650.

1876.	1877.	1878.	1879.
£135,710,420	£140,418,548	£121,663,920	£121,698,929

Average, £129,872,954.

Difference between the two periods, £16,712,696.

Imports of Chemicals and Dye-Stuffs.

1870.	1871.	1872.	1873.
£9,561,454	£10,500,894	£10,182,714	£9,734,875

Average, £9,995,234.

1876.	1877.	1878.	1879.
£9,634,877	£9,174,312	£9,109,561	£9,206,448

Average, £9,281,299.

Summary.

Average excess of imports over exports in	1870-1-2-3	£51,700,000
Average excess of imports over exports in	1876-7-8-6	£124,425,000

Classification of Imports.

Agricultural produce	£70,676,556 —	£100,362,007 +	£29,685,451
Manufactures ...	32,735,540 —	43,961,645 +	11,226,105
Raw materials ...	146,585,650 —	129,872,954 +	16,712,696
Chemicals, etc. ...	9,995,234 —	9,281,299 +	713,935[1]

Thus, in value, we imported less of raw material, such as cotton, flax, hemp, jute, hides, oil, silk, tallow, dyeing and tanning materials, which we are unable to produce, and more of agricultural products and manufactures coming into competition with our own industries.

What is the effect of all this? External competition is added to internal competition; the products of other lands, grown under more favourable conditions of labour and taxation, come into direct competition with our greatest industry—Agriculture; with our manufacturing industries, partially protected by labour laws, by Trade Unionism, by legislation exacted for the sole purpose of raising the condition of working

[1] These statistics, from official sources, were kindly compiled for me by Mr. H. F. Hibbert, F.S.S., of Chorley, Lancashire.

men from slavery to freedom, from ignorance to understanding, from misery to comfort, laws which, without
doubt, have raised the condition of our workers to a
higher social and moral position than those of any
other country in the world with the exception of the
United States of America, but which, nevertheless,
are a protection of labour against capital, with this
inevitable result :—In agriculture, the curtailment of
the spending power of landlords, tenants, and
labourers; in manufactures, the practical extinction of
some trades; in others, a low rate of remuneration to
capital, which if it were not for Trade Unionism, would
at once result in a drop in wages.

Now, what is the result of this low rate of remuneration to capital? (1) An absence of enterprise at
home; (2) an increase of foreign adventure; (3) a
diminished employment for the people in comparison
with the increase in our population; (4) increased
emigration returns. We are constantly being told
that our population is increasing at a more rapid rate
than our ability to maintain them, and therefore we
must devise some scheme to rid ourselves of that
which before long will become a burden to us. So,
we practically admit that we have reached the summit
of our prosperity, and that henceforth our position, as
an industrial nation, must be stationary, whilst other
nations, less favoured by natural resources, less
favoured in respect of genius and enterprise, and only
fractionally underpopulated in comparison with us,
march past us with rapid strides. This admission is
unworthy of a people with such a record as Great
Britain can boast of, and suggests the question—Have

we done all in our power as a nation to conserve and
develop the heritage to which we have succeeded ?

We must regretfully answer, No! We have
systematically thrown away that which is of the most
value to a nation—its *home market.* We have
neglected our colonies, which are the mainspring of
our commercial prosperity, and instead of attempting
to bind them together with the unbreakable chain of
self-interest, we have, in the past, neglected no opportunity of telling the world that they are an en-
cumbrance, with the inevitable result that the days
are rapidly passing away when any attempt at federation can be made with certainty as to the result.

Let us examine the matter from another point of
view.

In 1870 we exported of the produce and manufactures of the United Kingdom to the value of
£199,500,000, whilst we imported of similar produce
and manufactures from abroad £102,200,000, a difference of £97,300,000 in our favour. In 1886 we
exported, of similar produce, £212,400,000, whilst
we imported £158,600,000, a difference of only
£53,800,000 in our favour. Which was the prosperous
period ? Obviously the former. But Free Traders
would have us believe that we were more prosperous
in 1886, as, "the greater the excess of imports the
wealthier the nation, for it is the interest on your investments, your earnings from freight and insurance,
which comes home to you in the form of increased
imports." All very fine for the investor abroad ! But
we may ask, How is it we do not import raw cotton,
wool, oils, silk, and tallow, instead of oxen, sheep,

bacon, corn, beef, butter, eggs, and meat? We cannot produce the former; we do produce the latter. The answer is, Because under our present wretched system we cannot absorb the raw material.

We are forced to the conclusion that there is no relative expansion in our foreign trade, no elasticity in our home trade, that the British home market is glutted with foreign competing labour productions. Foreign nations prefer to send us manufactures to raw material; the production of the latter does not find sufficient employment for their people.

In proof of this contention, we, in 1870, imported raw material to the value of £158,100,000; in 1886 £150,300,000—decrease £7,800,000.

In 1870 we imported manufactures to the value of £42,200,000, in 1886 £68,500,000—*the enormous increase of £26,300,000.*

These are the plain unvarnished facts of the case; there is, comparatively speaking, no market for the raw material. We cannot absorb it, whilst agricultural produce and manufactures produced under more favourable conditions of labour and taxation find a ready sale.

If it is true that the greater the excess of imports over exports, the wealthier we become, if it is also true that this excess is entirely caused by increased imports of goods which *displace our labour*, it follows that the greater the displacement of labour in a country, the more prosperous is that country, and that it is more profitable for a nation to live on the interest of its capital with an occasional dip into the capital itself, than to augment the capital by the

addition of the interest on the same, plus the profits
gained during the year. Or, to simplify the matter,
a merchant is in a better way when, upon withdrawal
from business, he lives on the interest of his accumulated wealth, than he was in those years when he not
only had sufficient for his wants, but a large surplus
to invest ! Which is irrational.

The truth is, that in years gone by England's trade
was a profitable one, and the profits were largely invested abroad, resulting in the interests now extensively paid by the importation of competing labour
products. In those times the people were better
able to supply their own requirements, and capital
accumulated ; to-day, we are forced to spend accumulated capital on the very necessaries of life, and
our position as a nation is analogous to that of a
merchant, who, finding his profits less and his expenditure greater, is forced to draw from his banker
the accumulations of former years of prosperity, in
order to make ends meet. Who would say that the
merchant, under these circumstances, is in a better
way than when he not only paid his expenses out of
profits, but put aside a substantial reserve? Men
with business instincts can form their own conclu-
sions.

There is one branch of our imports and exports
which should not be left unnoticed—gold and silver
bullion and specie. It is a very complicated subject,
and difficult to deal with. It only totals a small
amount in comparison with the figures with which I
have been dealing in this chapter ; still it is too important a factor in our trade to be altogether omitted.

In relation to this it is significant that whereas, in our prosperous years of 1870-1-2-3, we imported £18,800,000 more than we exported, in 1876-7-8-9, years of depression, the balance between the two had dropped to £6,200,000; showing without doubt that the bullion we received in the former years, in *part* payment for our exports, had to be given up in the latter years in *part* payment of our enhanced imports, or, that instead of importing bullion we imported competing products or manufactures. Refuge is sometimes taken by Free Traders in the fact that a considerable portion of our imports are re-exported, that this intransitu trade finds employment for English ships and sailors, and the trades dependent upon the shipping industry, and, therefore, is a source of wealth to us.

But in the two periods of years which we have had under examination, years of prosperity and years of depression; years of small and years of great difference between imports and exports, our re-export trade was practically at a standstill, being on an average £54,793,000 during the former, and £54,869,000 for the latter period.

The re-export trade of recent years shows declension rather than expansion; the total for the twelve months ending August 31st, 1894, was £56,018,842, compared with £63,993,841 for the same time ending August 31st, 1893. Even when we allow for the increased purchasing power of gold, the returns with former years of our re-exports show a decline when compared. It is remarkable that in the face of statistics, such as I present in this chapter, any one should hold to the doctrine that "every import necessitates an equal export"; Englishmen have not followed the actual experiences of life in trade matters, but have remained spellbound to the theories of Free Trade. It is a pity that so many educated people in this country stoutly refuse to examine the position; far better to get at the naked facts.

Mr. Sampson S. Lloyd some years ago, in a letter to *The Times*, stated the position very clearly by asking :—"Can a nation, any more than a family or individual, continue to purchase more than it sells, and to consume more than it produces, with safety to the permanent interests of the masses who live by labour?" Emphatically No! The true mainspring of prosperity and wealth is employment. And how can our working people have full, varied, and profitable employment when they do not possess the British home market? All who are able to distinguish clearly, without party bias, from an absolutely neutral position, and with judicial instincts, must be forced to this conclusion, namely, that our inflated import trade, by displacing the labour of our people, must impoverish the country to the extent of the labour displaced, and that if we continue to import from abroad that which we could, and ought to, produce at home, we are slowly, but surely, hastening the day when our producing power will be so exhausted that we shall have no choice left for the workers but to emigrate or starve.

We have seen that the excess is largely paid for by our profits from investments in foreign countries, *viz.*, bonds, land, railways, public works, manufactories, etc., and that this means that these foreign earnings take the place of the earnings which should result from the products of British labour—because of the displacement of home production for home consumption.

Capital saved in bygone years has been called "dead men's profits or wages," and so the imports from alien States of agricultural produce, which we ought to (and formerly did) produce at home, and imports of foreign competing manufactured goods, are made available to pay promptly the "interests" on "*dead men's earnings.*" [1]

Result—Loss of British home market; labour impoverished; and, finally, working-men—the bone and sinew of the country—sent across the ocean to seek that employment which the fiscal laws of this country prevent them from obtaining at home.

Are we to regard the interests of the capitalist—with a ready-made income—in preference to the interests of the great mass of the population, who need full employment to enable them to live? No; the prosperity of the country depends upon imports being paid for by *live men's earnings,* and we shall find out in time that working people cannot consume the cheap foreign productions without the means of purchase, that is, the command of wages—the "Sunday's dinner" depends upon the "Saturday night's pay."

Doubtless there are other ways—minor avenues—in which the "excess" is paid for—namely, the profits

---

[1] Thus the "few" are benefited, but the "many" are injured.

on the carrying trade, freights earned by British ships and insurance, also by the transfer of securities.

"The profits of the carrying trade" is one of the chief weapons in the Free Trade armoury.

British shipping is an industry which has made continuous progress until recently, but whatever success has attended it in the past has been no compensation for the distress caused to home production by an unfair fiscal system. As a people we may congratulate ourselves as "ocean carriers," but we must not forget our ruined agriculture, and the collapse of many home industries. The wealth of a country is the value of what it produces. Are the profits of the carrying trade compensation for throwing over 1,000,000 acres out of wheat cultivation during recent years, for impoverishing stock and dairy farming, and for making our immense manufacturing capital unremunerative, and rendering the employment of our artisans and operatives uncertain and spasmodic?

We may enumerate, reiterate, and exaggerate the profits of the carrying trade, but do not let us pass over the ruin of millions of native producers.

Free Trade economists may assert till they are black in the face as to how the adverse balance is paid, but it is certainly not paid by the profits in the carrying trade.

There are many reasons—political, historical, and geographical—to account for England's pre-eminence on the high seas, and we have natural advantages in the building of ships—the possession of coal and iron near the sea-board, with the needed labour—besides the fact that since England became a great nation she has exceeded other nations in her shipping enterprise. But I do not propose to enter upon the consideration of these questions; my subject now is one of freights and profits to liquidate the adverse balance, and this concerns us as a nation so far as the profits earned by British ships, *the net profits*, that is, such portion of this total as is not spent abroad in working the ships. Sometimes the receipts (profits in the *foreign* carrying trade) are put down at £40 millions per annum; the shipowners of this country would be delighted to find the statement true!

I leave the calculation of net profits, earned to-day, to British shipowners; their estimate will be a very moderate one. Speaking broadly, *it is a time for estimating losses*—not profits.

As to insurance and interest on advances, some people say so many millions, and others so much more. I will not venture upon an estimate.

Lastly, the transfer of securities. Namely, THE TRANSFER TO FOREIGNERS OF ENGLISH FUNDS AND STOCK, ALSO THE RE-SALE TO FOREIGNERS OF FOREIGN FUNDS AND STOCK PREVIOUSLY HELD IN THIS COUNTRY. We have no statistical returns of these transactions. At the same time there is a general belief that British securities have, during recent years, changed hands to the foreigner, as well as amounts of foreign securities re-transferred. We may reasonably conclude that some portion (it may be a small one) of the excess of imports over exports is paid for in this way.

It is the contention of some of the less educated

H

classes that the excess of imports over exports goes
to show that, in the course of trade under our present
policy, we are getting more than we give. Thus, they
would say, "We export £10 worth of British production, and we get in exchange for it, say, £20 worth
of foreign. Therefore, we have a national profit of
100 per cent." Out of Bedlam, was there ever such
an idiotic delusion cherished and expressed? To
demolish such an absurd belief, we have only to apply
the *reductio ad absurdum* illustration. If, when our
imports exceed our exports by 100 per cent., we
have a national profit of 100 per cent., what would
our profit be—with equal imports—if we had no exports at all? The fools forget that imports have got
to be paid for to the full amount of their value; that
they are consumed, not exchanged. If their contention were true, the alleged "national profit" would be
reflected in excess exports, or, further, investments
abroad, or reduced taxation; and then—and then
only—would good business be done.

Besides, the truth of the matter may be demonstrated to the common intelligence in another way.
The nominal money-value upon the national invoice,
either of ourselves or the foreigner, is not the real or
cost value, but the *exchange* value of the goods sold
or bought. Supposing the contention of these ignorant people were a fact, that, for every sale of home
production costing us £10, we received in exchange
£20 worth of foreign production, then, our invoice to
the foreigner would bear the value expressed as £20,
not £10, and his to us would bear the value of £10,
not £20.

Were we, in reality, getting more in the course of trade than we gave, either our exports would be to the full amount of the difference in excess of our imports, or we should be receiving from the foreigner a composite settlement, *viz.*, value for value, *plus* the interest upon money lent, and other charges. For example, the accounts, as they actually stand between John Bull and the foreigner are somewhat as under :—

F. *Dr.* to J. B.		J. B. *Dr.* to F.	
To Cash, Interests on Investments, Freights, etc. ..	£10 0 0	To Goods	£20 0 0
To Goods	10 0 0		
	£20 0 0		£20 0 0

If goods exported were really being paid for by goods imported, the accounts would stand thus :—

F. *Dr.* to J. B.		J. B. *Dr.* to F.	
To Cash, Interests on Investments, Freights, etc. ..	£10 0 0	To Goods	£20 0 0
To Goods	20 0 0	To Cash, Securities, etc., remitted (to balance) ..	10 0 0
	£30 0 0		£30 0 0

If goods were being exported in excess of goods imported, the accounts would stand as follows :—

F. *Dr.* to J. B.		J. B. *Dr.* to F.	
To Cash, Interests on Investments, Freights, etc. ..	£10 0 0	To Goods	£20 0 0
To Goods	30 0 0	To Cash, Securities remitted or transferred	10 0 0
		To " I. O. U.'s "	10 0 0
	£40 0 0		£40 0 0

Table showing the Progressive Excess of Imports over Exports.

Net Imports. (Imports less Re-Exports.)			Exports of British and Irish Produce.			Excess of Imports over Exports
Years.	Amount. Million £	Amount per Head. £ s. d.	Years.	Amount. Million £	Amount per Head. £ s. d.	Million £
1860	181		1860	136		
1861	182		1861	125		
1862	184		1862	124		
1863	199		1863	147		
1864	223		1864	160		
Anl. Avg. 1860-4.	193	6 12 9		138	4 14 8	55
1865	218		1865	166		
1866	245		1866	189		
1867	230		1867	181		
1868	247		1868	179		
1869	248		1869	190		
Anl. Avg. 1865-9.	237	7 16 3		181	5 19 0	56
1870	259		1870	200		
1871	270		1871	223		
1872	297		1872	256		
1873	315		1873	255		
1874	312		1874	240		
Anl. Avg. 1870-4.	291	9 2 4		235	7 7 3	56
1875	316		1875	223		
1876	319		1876	201		
1877	340		1877	199		
1878	317		1878	193		
1879	306		1879	192		
Anl. Avg. 1875-9.	320	9 10 4		202	6 0 0	118
1880	348		1880	223		
1881	334		1881	234		
1882	348		1882	242		
1883	362		1883	240		
1884	327		1884	233		
Anl. Avg. 1880-4.	344	9 14 9		234	6 12 9	110
1885	313		1885	213		
1886	294		1886	213		
1887	303		1887	222		
1888	324		1888	234		
1889	360		1889	249		
Anl. Avg. 1885-9.	318	8 11 11		226	6 2 0	92
1890	356		1890	263[1]		
1891	373		1891	247		
1892	359		1892	227		
1893	346		1893	218[1]	..	

[1] The declension in the values of the exports of British and Irish produce—1890 compared with 1893—is very remarkable.

CHAPTER IX.

FANATICISM IN POLITICS AND POLITICAL ECONOMY —FREE TRADE PREDESTINARIANS, AND THEIR IDOLATRY.

Political Wire-pulling — " Great is Gladstone ! " — Political Parties—The Politicians' Charm—" Pious Aspirations " of the Conservatives, 1884-5—Political Wrangling—Mr. John Bright substituting " Cheap " for " Exchange "—A Gathering Storm.

THE country is divided into two political parties ; these parties are constantly striving for the mastery, backed by political organisation ; political organisation is dependent upon political sagacity, and political sagacity consists of securing votes by successfully wire-pulling the electorate.

Governments are made, and governments are kept alive, by majorities of votes.[1] Just now Mr. Gladstone is the political idol of one party, a party the reverse of homogeneous. Mr. Gladstone has enough to do to keep all the worshippers bowing down ; in fact, his mind is continually occupied with thoughts of how the wonderfully constituted party can be kept together. To this end a good many promises are made ; bribes are offered, and fawning and flattering is the order of the day. Yet, there he stands, and the de-

[1] Written before Mr. Gladstone's resignation of office.

votees proclaim, " The greatest living man "—great is
Gladstone !

The Tory party no longer exists.   The Tories did
not keep to their own peculiar province; they "dished"
the Whigs and Radicals with a Reform Bill, they
have passed Free Education, and generally spread
abroad political bird-lime quite as freely as the other
party.   At election times the generic term Free
Trade has been something to conjure with, the cry of
the " big loaf," the " cheap loaf," has been turned
to advantage, and so both political parties have ex-
pounded the creed of *laissez-faire.*

It is true that the Home Rule Bill of Mr. Gladstone has brought about a new political combination,
Liberal-Unionists uniting with Conservatives; but
outside of the Irish question, and their mutual adherence to *laissez-faire,* in matters of trade policy
there is very little agreement, certainly none as regards the social and labour problems which will very
shortly demand attention.

The mischief of unregulated foreign competition in
the British market is causing a commotion; the wage-
earner is fast reckoning up the consequences of free
competing imports as bearing down his employment
and wages.   Politicians have, in the past, pacified
the workers by giving them votes, consequently the
democratic current is fairly in motion — leading
where?   Not in the direction of the politicians'
economic orthodoxy, but to higher wages and the
restriction of external competition.

The democracy bluntly denounce the pretensions
of political economy, and evince a burning desire to

substitute for the creed of *laissez-faire* the claims of humanity.

At one time (when Trade Unionism did not exist) the Free Trade catechism was the politicians' charm, and people possessed an almost superstitious reverence for the authors of the catechism ; this was the leaps and bounds period, when the wise men were almost worshipped. No wonder that politicians took up the charm. Well, the special causes, giving an impetus to British trade, passed away ; circumstances changed, for instead of England doing work for foreign countries the latter found a good market in this country for their own labour products—foods and goods.

This external competition in our markets has gone on year by year, and has resulted in British acres going out of cultivation, and British manufactures being superseded by foreign manufactures ; not only so, but foreign markets have been year by year closing upon us under a system of scientific protection, designed to further the interests of native labour. For a generation Englishmen have been absolutely spellbound by certain theories of trade, so much so, that many of our leading men in the political world have resolutely refused to examine our fiscal system, sufficient for them the declaration "that our Free Trade policy does not allow of any import duties being imposed on such articles as are produced at home." How this position can satisfy reasonable men, men with business instincts, is a mystery, so much is the idol of free imports worshipped in this country.

The naked fact, however, is that the project of 1846 is a dream; the international exchange of products, so much insisted upon by Mr. Cobden, has not taken place. Why contend that the country has been blessed by a system which has never even been tried ?

Lord Salisbury's Government of 1885 appointed a Royal Commission to investigate the depression of trade, and (to use Lord Salisbury's words) "to find out what legislative modifications of it can be discovered."

The appointment of this Royal Commission was bitterly opposed by the Liberals, who resented it as an attack upon the holy and sacred principles of Free Trade. The most superficial observer of political movements during the past forty years must come to the conclusion that Free Trade has been the base of the politicians' power—their sacred religion ; only let a poor fellow be caught in the act of throwing stones at the image, the vials of wrath are poured out and a great cry arises—Great is Diana !

Yes, ask for bare justice to British industries by the consideration of fiscal duties, and you are accused of " economical heresy."

Conservatives, during 1884-5, took up the cry of " Bad Trade," and professed to have pious aspirations upon the question of supporting British industries. *One-sided* Free Trade was viewed with dissatisfaction. This attitude of the Conservative party was met by the Radicals with an exhibition of the scarecrow—the " dear loaf," and the wickedness of taxing " the food of the people."

Nothing was said of the burden of taxation on the food produced at home. Nothing was said of the value of home production and domestic exchanges, compared with foreign production and foreign exchanges, that "foreign trade is but the handmaid of home trade."

Conservatives in office are different beings to Conservatives in opposition, for during the late administration the leaders of the party dropped the cause of fiscal reform. True, the rank and file now and then kindled a little flame, only to be extinguished by command. We all know of the political wrangling over Irish affairs since Mr. Gladstone undertook to dispense salvation to Separatists. Let this pass, for the Irish question is falling into the background, eclipsed by social and labour problems and matters of Imperial consequence. Free Traders and politicians can shift their positions with marvellous rapidity. It is difficult to contemplate the developments in store for us in the near future. Here is an example of Mr. John Bright substituting "cheap" for "exchange." Mr. Bright wrote to a correspondent in 1885, "that to imagine that your suffering springs now from hostile tariffs is absurd." Contrast this declaration with what the same gentleman said in a speech delivered at Liskeard, on the 15th April, 1843:—"One-half of the people in Sheffield, in Birmingham, and other large towns, are employed in working on articles which are sold abroad! but in consequence of our refusing in this country to take the productions of foreign soil, foreigners refuse to take our goods except under very disadvantageous

circumstances. They place very high import duties
on goods taken into their countries, so high that we
are unable to sell in those countries, *except by beating
down wages at home.*"   In 1843 Mr. Bright was looking to the "free exchange of untaxed commodities,"
whereas in 1885 his Free Trade had resolved itself
into simply *cheap buying from abroad free from
taxation*—" the inestimable advantages of cheap buying."   The reader can judge where the absurdity
comes in.   If the foreign consumer paid the full
amount of the tariff imposed, why should Mr. Bright
have spoken about "beating down the wages" of
Englishmen to enable exporters to overcome foreign
tariffs ?   If this was the position in 1843 it is much
more so in 1894—for internal production in foreign
countries has enormously increased, and foreign tariffs
have greatly advanced.   British labour has suffered in
consequence.

Free Trade has deprived us of our bargaining
power, and the sooner the working classes of this
country take the situation to heart, and break through
party allegiance, the better it will be for them.
When this position is reached it will be in vain for
politicians to dogmatise and cover themselves with
the cloak of Free Trade infallibility, for they and
the theoretical professors of the dismal science will
be sternly bidden to stand aside.

Holy Free Trade will be discounted, and the delusion exposed.

The rumbling we hear to-day in labour circles—the
democracy protesting against ruthless competition
with populations that work long hours and for low

wages—protesting against an overplus foreign supply of competing labour products—protesting against the doctrine of " the devil take the hindmost "—these are indications of the gathering storm.

Free Trade (grim Moloch !) is swamping the home market with the products of foreign labour.

CHAPTER X.

IRELAND UNDER FREE TRADE DISTRESSED AND
DISAFFECTED—IRELAND'S REAL NEED.

Justice to Ireland—Ireland's Material Wrongs—Mr. Parnell's
Declaration and Demand—Ireland's Industrial Interests—
A Monument to the Folly of the "Let Alone," Chapter
of Accidents Policy—Extermination or Banishment—The
Strongest Link—Climbing the Slippery Hill-side of Home
Rule—If the Tory Party had Political Sense—Quack
Remedies—John Bull as a Miserable Sinner.

POOR Ireland! Poor John Bull! Both afflicted
politically and economically.

The history of Ireland is a record of conspiracy,
rebellion, agitation, confiscation, penal laws, religious
intolerance, tyranny, commercial restrictions, misery,
resentment, and ill-will. It is beyond the power of
the writer, and the space at his disposal in this
chapter, to take up and examine the course of
government in Ireland, before and after the Union;
the character of the Irish people—their habits, religious
and educational ideas, and their political champions;
the tenure of land, and all that is summed up in the
phrase, "Justice to Ireland"—a phrase so liberally
used by the Gladstonian party during the last twenty-
five years. It is not the place to review the measures
passed by Mr. Gladstone, and the political agitation

carried on, during recent years, under the cry of
" Justice to Ireland."

But it may not be out of place to look at Ireland's
material wrongs, suffered since the Act of Union,
and, in this connection, the following utterance of the
late Mr. Parnell (claiming self-government for Ireland)
is to the point :—" I claim for Ireland that if the Irish
Parliament of the future considers there are certain
industries in Ireland which can be benefited by Protection, which can be nursed by Protection, and which
can be placed in such a position as to enable them to
compete with similar industries in other countries by
a course of Protection over a few years, Parliament
ought to have the power to carry out that policy; and
I tell English Radicals and English Liberals that it
is useless for them to talk of their desire to do justice
to Ireland when, with motives of selfishness, they refused to repair that most manifest injustice of all—
the destruction of our manufactures by England in
times past."

It is evident that Mr. Parnell's demand for justice
required that Ireland should have Protection.

The successors of Mr. Parnell have dropped the
demand of their late lamented chief; their presently
expressed ideas of " Ireland a nation " do not include
fiscal liberty—one of the first principles of nationality.
Mr. Justin M'Carthy and his backers withdrew from
doing wrong to Mr. Gladstone's party and the
members of the Cobden Club. Irish patriotism, as
represented to-day at St. Stephen's, refrains from laying violent hands upon the idol Free Trade. This
position is a distinct warning to those who profess to

believe in the finality of Mr. Gladstone's Bill; in truth, there is no finality about it.

Whatever may be the evils of Ireland, they will never be cured without a proper consideration being paid to Ireland's industrial interests. The people require employment, and if this is secured, agitation will disappear. Employment for Irishmen will never be created under the present hollow notions of political economy.

The agricultural position of the country is a rebuke to Free Trade. It may be asked, Are not Irishmen themselves responsible for the introduction of the policy of free competing imports? Yes. O'Connell and his followers enabled Cobden and Sir Robert Peel to carry one-sided Free Trade. This is a matter of history.

Ireland's millions of acres of uncultivated land, her ruined manufactures and commerce, her half-starving people, and her landed proprietors, testify to the consequences of Free Trade. The condition of Ireland is a monument to the folly of the "let alone" policy, or leaving things to the chapter of accidents (the Bible of the fool). Will politicians admit the palpable failure? It is quite clear that since the date of the Union, during the first forty years, English competition ruined Ireland's mechanical industries, and since England adopted free imports, Ireland has found, year by year, the cultivation of her soil more and more unprofitable; particularly since 1874 has foreign produce been substituted for that of her own fields. Ireland has suffered more than England. Why? Because Ireland, not having the varied industrial interests and accumulated capital of England, is more dependent on the produce of the soil; Ireland has keenly felt the depreciation in values of agricultural produce, hence the general disaffection and war against landlords and rent.

No reasonable man can doubt that free imports have brought about the decay of agriculture in Ireland, and are the cause of her being rapidly depopulated. We cannot wonder at people threatened with extermination or banishment being disaffected, and giving themselves up to agitators, who promise to govern according to the wants of the country.

The depopulation of Ireland cries shame upon our fiscal system.[1]

However, the dismemberment of the empire is no remedy for Ireland's troubles. The true remedy is to give up Free Trade idolatry, and support a national policy of safeguarding our Imperial and industrial interests ; build upon the foundation of a united empire, demonstrate to the whole world the strength of the British Empire, commercially and politically.

With a policy of work and wages discontent will pass away, and there will be no need for an Irish Parliament. Ireland will then awake to new life, and dismiss Separatists and sham patriots, and Englishmen, too, will turn with contempt and loathing upon those unstable turn-coat politicians, who, for love of power and greed of office, have not hesitated to league themselves with men preaching the doctrine of public plunder, and intent upon breaking down

_____

[1] See Chapter XVIII., " Emigration," p. 197.

the authority of Parliament, and seeking the dismemberment of the British Empire.

The salvation of poor, disorganised Ireland can never be brought about by the most unstable statesman of this or any other age, who has only succeeded in making confusion worse confounded.

It is to be regretted that the late Unionist government did not adopt a bold line of action, and so eclipse the machinations of the Home Rule agitation —an evil and artful design—by taking up the cause of native labour, and the policy of Imperial commercial federation—the strongest link in welding together a kingdom and an empire. To have entered upon this magnificent policy, which is right, and true, and sound, would have infused vigour into our national life, and proved the determination to redress the wrongs from which both agriculture and manufactures are now suffering in Great Britain and Ireland. To have dealt with the responsibilities of the mother country to her colonies, to have considered the claims and necessities of the whole empire, would have secured a prestige in marked contra-distinction to a parochial peddling over the question of Home Rule for Ireland. Yes, to have fought the parochial programme of Mr. Gladstone, and his time-serving following, with a grand Imperial policy, would have been safe and dignified.

What stood in the way of this consummation ? A false theory—Free Trade. The present political situation is but the sequel to the anti-colonial and other cosmopolitan theories of Cobdenite politicians.

[1] The Gladstonian Disruptionist Government are climbing the slippery hillside of Home Rule, and it looks as if they will, before long, fall headlong to the bottom; further, this time-serving government appears to be losing any temporary cohesion, even for mischief, that they possess, and are going to pieces in a general scramble for local and parochial dishonesties. We may take heart, for it is possible that a great *need* may find a great national expression by force of circumstances, and so Home Rule may be finally shelved, and *Irish Protectionists be found uniting with patriotic Englishmen for the sake of a protective policy.*

If the Tory party—or what remains of it—had political sense, it would, at this juncture, join the fiscal question—Protection to Trade and Empire—to the Irish question.

Depend upon it that the disestablishment of churches and confiscation of endowments, penalising of landlords, Home Rule and no rent policies and manifestoes, parish councils, allotments, small holdings, eight hours bills, and free this and free the other thing, are but quack remedies—pills to cure an industrial earthquake.

We have smothered Ireland's agriculture by free imports, and her people will never be induced to work on the land without a system of wise national protection ; this is the true remedy for Irish misery, discontent and insubordination.

Let John Bull (as a miserable sinner) admit that he has done wrong, repent, and *make restitution;* let

---

[1] Written before Mr. Gladstone's resignation of office.

him place Ireland on a true and actual level with England by the protection of British and Irish industries.

Yes, John Bull should emulate the Hebrew king
who fell upon his face in sackcloth, and cried : " I
have sinned and done evil ; but these sheep, what have
they done ? Let Thy hand, O Lord my God, be on
me and on my father's house, and not on my people,
that they should be plagued."

CHAPTER XI.

" CHEAPNESS."

COMPETITION AND HONESTY.

The " Great Mogul "—Honesty thrown to the Winds—The Tricks of Trade—" Limited " Companies—A Fine Art of how not to do it—" Raising the Wind "—" Cheapness " not a Sign of Prosperity—Miry Fallacies—The Hypocrisy of " Free Traders."

IT has been said " The world is governed by words." Mr. Goschen gives another version, namely, " The country is to a great extent governed and influenced by phrases." Verily, in modern times, there is no word more seductive, more beguiling, than " cheap." It is the Great Mogul of the system, which has for over forty years appealed to the cupidity of our people, fashioning their every desire, directing every action ; in fact, it has subjugated popular opinion in every direction.

Cheapness has been the god of this generation. Many sacrifices have been made to its shrine ; the foundations of society are undermined in the scramble for obtaining commodities cheap—cheaper than they can honestly be produced. Unrestricted competition is a premium on dishonesty and villainy ; adulteration is rampant, tainting every branch of business, and

lowering national life. Goods are made to appear
what they are not; worthless articles are ticketed
"cheap," and honesty is thrown to the winds.

In former years, tables and chairs were tables and
chairs—made for use, made with the best materials
and the best workmanship, as good as they could be,
serviceable articles, bespeaking excellence of quality,
and handed down with pride from one generation to
another. Now they are made for show and deception, to please the unwary.

Various imitations of butter have taken the place
of the real article ; genuine lard is difficult to procure ;
shoddy is sold for woollen cloth ; cotton cloth is produced to imitate flannel (flannelette) ; soft iron for
steel ; hemp and cotton for silk ; coloured compounds
for wine ; starchy beet-root as sugar from the sugar-
cane ; foreign meat has taken the place of " the roast-
beef of Old England " ; soap is made with a very
limited quantity of tallow, but loaded with cheap
chemicals ; leather is not worthy the name, and boots
are not made for wear ; vile rubbish is sold for tea ;
Dutch metal passes as gold-leaf; Swedish pauper-
made laths have taken the place of well-seasoned,
well-made, English laths ; jerry houses spring up like
mushrooms. Truly, we have cheapness, and nastiness.

Inferior articles are substituted for the good ; our
markets are flooded with rubbish ; " good old houses
of business are driven into evil courses to keep their
place in the race, and underbid their rivals ; reputa-
tions acquired by honest work are recklessly squandered "—in the demand for cheapness.

Concerns are converted into limited companies to

enable old proprietors to clear out; " they have served their turn, and they are indifferent as to what comes after them." With the lump of realised capital (frequently re-invested in foreign countries) they can live in luxury. It may be in London, or periodically enjoying the scenery of the Maritime Alps, or in palatial residences, with the usual accessories of hot-houses, vineries, pineries, and orchid cultivation. " They are but representatives of a spendthrift nation, living upon its capital ! "

In transacting business nowadays, the good old method of promptly discharging obligations is turned into a fine art of how not to do it; keeping Peter waiting to satisfy the demands of Paul; decorating (" crossing " and to " order ") cheques to prevent immediate presentation, " post date " them, stave off the time, in the hope of somehow raising the wind to obtain money to place in the bank in time they (the cheques) get back for payment, etc.

Instead of probity and intelligence, we witness in many directions swindling, roguery, and selfishness. Liquidators make a rich harvest out of bankrupt estates. " Assets realisation " companies have sprung up right and left to drive a thriving business out of the wreck and ruin, conveniently taking over from bankers their " white elephants," upon which advances have been made to impecunious clients. With limited companies, trading has been carried on to give a nominal interest upon subscribed capital. The mania for creating limited companies has nourished a spirit of gambling; capital is subscribed, not as a permanent investment, but to snatch a premium.

The whole system of limited liability requires a
complete investigation.   It would be instructive if
Parliament would furnish a return of all companies
which have gone into liquidation, giving the total
amount of capital called up—and lost.

Reckless trading is the order of the day—trading
without reasonable profits.   Now, if the trader has
not a margin of profit on his turn-over to cover the
standing expenses, it is as sure as the multiplication
table that that style of business will absorb his capital,
i.e., if he has any.   If he is trading without capital,
then his creditors' capital will be absorbed.   Well,
all this is simply transferring capital from one class
to another; the nation is none the poorer.   The nation
is impoverished *when production does not go on*, for a
nation's wealth consists in its production ; it is the
falling away of the wages of labour which lessens the
wealth fund of the nation.   The workers form the
bulk of the nation.   When they earn good wages, and
get full employment, they create, by what they consume, an immense home market.

Cheapness is not a sign of prosperity.   Whenever
did we have prosperity with low prices?   High wages
and   low-priced   commodities   are   not   compatible.
Cheap goods mean low wages.   If we recall the state
of things over twenty years ago, when (owing to the
Franco-German War) production went on rapidly in
this country, when work was plentiful for all, we did
not rave about cheapness.   Landlords received large
rents ; the occupier of the soil did well ; labourers
were busy in the fields ; operatives were going full
time in our mills and workshops.   Were these times

of cheapness? Certainly not. The working man paid
7d. and 8d. for his 4lb. loaf without grumbling. He
had money to buy it, and to spare. The poor old
woman insisted upon having best tea, at 4s. per
pound; best butter only was sold (there was no
imitations of butter); people would only take the
best bacon, and other provisions. These were days
of high prices, but *real cheapness*, because of the
ability to purchase.

What the masses want is not nominal cheapness,
but the means of purchase. Without this, it is a
matter of supreme indifference to them how cheap
commodities may be.

The full and varied productive employment of the
people is the true sign of a nation's prosperity.

The glut of cheap foreign productions in our
markets destroys the means of purchase to our
workers. It restricts home productions, renders fixed
capital profitless, and destroys the wages of labour.
The cheapness of the recent years is attained by low
and inadequate wages, hence the sweating system, as
it exists with all unorganised workers. It is only by
Trade Unions that wages have been maintained, and
this often at the expense of capital.

Let Free Traders always remember that Trade
Unionism is the most severe form of protection.[1]

[1] Cheap food was intended to give our manufacturers cheap
labour, to enable them to maintain a supremacy in foreign
markets; but Free Trade manufacturers did not bargain for
foreign tariffs (forcing down the prices of their goods and
diminishing profits) and Trade Unionism keeping up the operatives' wages.

It is a common thing for Free Traders to support Trade

Untaxed foreign goods, the produce of cheap labour
and long hours, when imported into this country,
must bring down profits and wages. It is an artificially constituted competition forced upon our workers,
displacing their labour and bringing down the rate of
wages.

After the glut of cheapness comes the check, owing
to restricted or displaced home production for home
consumption ; then our workers know by painful experience that the boasted cheapness is a suicidal
cheapness. The fact is, if we consume food and buy
goods which have not paid their fair quota towards
the taxation of the country, they are dear at any
price—from a national point of view. It is no use
talking about "the inestimable advantages of cheap
buying," without being informed how people are to
buy without money.

We have seen that cheapness is the result of low
and inadequate wages of labour, and that under a
system of free competing imports the competition of
the world is centred in our markets, that it turns upon
cheap labour, *i.e.*, competition in flesh and blood.

"The survival of the cheapest" is the fundamental
doctrine of Free Trade, and the devotees of the
system are so crammed with sophisms that they
flounder about in all sorts of miry fallacies. With
many it will be a considerable time before they know
the measure of their folly.

Unionism as a good thing. *John Bright did not.* Surely their
raison d'être is to regulate, to restrain competition. "The con-
tradictions and inconsistencies of Free Trade are indeed
perplexing."

We are often told Free Trade is good because it gives a high remuneration of labour. It does nothing of the sort. The doctrine of low prices has been preached as the one thing needful. We are supposed to go down on our knees and say, "Thank God, everything is very cheap!" At the same time, Free Traders, in their hearts, want to raise prices. Such is the hypocrisy of the system.

CHAPTER XII.

THE subject of this chapter is of vast importance, demanding most careful consideration.

"Take care of the consumer" is the leading
maxim, fixed and stereotyped, of the Free Trade
school ; it is an exhortation to grasp, frantically
grasp, at cheapness—get it anyhow. " Take care of
the consumer" is the doctrine which appeals so
effectually to the cupidity of the individual ; it is a
gloating over a low value of commodities without
any regard to the conditions under which they are
produced and obtained. Therefore, we may infer
that, "Take care of the consumer" means looking
after the interest of the individual, and overlooking
the interests of the community. The reader may
say, Is not the last statement a contradiction ? Are
we not looking after the community when speaking
of the welfare of the consumer ? Well, all live by

and on production, and a very large proportion of the people, probably four-fifths, must have the means of purchase, by selling their labour, before they can purchase.

It must always be remembered, and it cannot be too often stated, that not only is every producer a consumer, but there is not a consumer who is not either a producer or else living entirely out of the income of a producer, or past production, from the Queen of England to the meanest beggar in the street.

Landlords live upon rent—when they are fortunate enough to get it; tenants live upon profits, and labourers live upon wages—all the revenue of producers. Professional people too—lawyers, doctors, parsons, etc., are ultimately paid by the producers. All these classes thrive when production takes place under prosperous conditions. On the other hand, they suffer when producers are injured.

All must agree that production is the only source of national wealth, and whatever militates against the development of national production injures the whole community. We have the authority of Adam Smith for this conclusion in his statement :—

" A nation, whether it consume its own productions, or with them purchase from abroad, can have no more to spend than it produces. Therefore, the supreme policy of every nation is to develop its own producing forces."

What are the producing forces of our country? The land, the working population, the mines, the machinery, which we possess. Develop all these

forces and the nation will have ample revenue,
sufficient to pay taxation incident to consumers, and
more, surplus revenue for the whole community to
spend and enjoy. An old writer, referring to this
point, says :—

"Nay, the very tax itself will, in most cases, soon
disappear; for the development of your own producing power will not only, at first and at once, bring
plenty and riches, but in the end will bring a steady
cheapness too, and along with that cheapness the
powers of purchasing. It will add accessibility to
cheapness."

It is necessary for the Free Trade argument to
construct broad lines of distinction between producers and consumers—to constitute the nation into
two hostile camps ; however, the distinction has
very little existence in fact.

We have seen that every member of the community is a consumer; there are those who are
exclusively consumers, people with ready-made incomes, living upon the interests of accumulated
capital, but a large majority are *both producers* and
consumers. The large majority includes the labourer,
who has but his labour to sell; and when the foreigner
steps in to secure our good home market, without
paying any part of our national working expenses,
then *native labour is sacrificed.* Why? Because
that labour is handicapped with taxation.

The home producer has a natural right to his
market, and the first chance of it. National Protection would restore that right which Free Trade has
deprived him of.

The working man cannot buy till he sells, and what does he sell? His labour. It is no possible use to the working classes of England to buy competing labour products from abroad, free from taxation, simply in order to depreciate the products of native labour, for by so doing they suffer in their capacity of consumers; *i.e.*, their ability to purchase is diminished; there is less to spend all round, and we get bad trade.

If native labour is invaded, its value is reduced. We are aware, from actual experience, that low-priced, untaxed, foreign corn has destroyed the labour and profits of British agriculture, and pushed our overtaxed corn out of cultivation. The same process is going on as regards British manufactures. Why this devastation? To save the consumer from paying his quota to imperial and local taxation. But see, all ye who uphold the presumptuous and dangerous policy of unbridled foreign competition, how the *producer is sacrificed*, and the *nation impoverished*.

Cheap foreign foods, goods, and luxuries, suit people with ready-made incomes; economy in expenditure is a fine thing for them (selfish beings); but the tax collector comes round, exacting money from the producers, the labourers' wages are sacrificed, and, finally, he loses his employment.

"Take care of the consumer" is sheer folly, for we (the nation) lose more than we gain *i.e.*, the individual may gain in expenditure, but *the nation loses in revenue*.

Trade is carried on for profit; when the collection

of taxes and foreign competition presses unduly on
trade, profit disappears; there is no enterprise, and
consequently no employment.

We may have reduced prices, but we gain nothing;
the values of everything come down, and the means
of buying are reduced.

In the previous chapter, cheapness is referred to as
the Free Trade god.   Briefly, What does cheapness
really mean?   Cheapness of production, which involves cheapness of labour, and cheapness of labour
means degradation for all who live as wage earners.
In fact, the cheapness arising from commodities
secured by low wages of labour is, to be logical, a
contradiction in terms.   It means giving six to five,
five to four, four to three, and so on, to round O.   If
this cheapness is an advantage, a blessing to our industrial population, if it is a good thing as an end
per se, therefore we may argue that when food products and textiles and manufactures generally can be
produced at half the present price, it were better to
get these products of labour at half these prices, and
better still if secured at a quarter their values.   Well,
at the lowest scale of prices, production could not
possibly go on, neither could we have the means to
import.   Yes, Englishmen have made cheapness into
a god, or goddess, and placed her, as the Romans did
Fortune, in Heaven, whereas if we had done the reverse, and banished her to a lower sphere, it would
have been better for us all.

Cheapness is a very questionable policy for the proletariat of any country which reserves its markets for
the industry of its own producers.   It is an undoubted

temporary advantage to one class alone, namely, the capitalistic idle class who inherit and live upon inherited fortunes. The only sphere where cheapness is a possible national advantage is where some great invention or accession of productive resources simplifies and accelerates the processes of production and distribution, and enables the same amount of capital and labour to earn more frequent returns and greater results.

This gain—obtained and obtainable in this way alone—is compatible with enhanced wages to workers, greater profits to capitalists and middlemen, but only in competition with the trade of some other communities who have not got the advantage of these conditions. In order, therefore, for even this form of cheapness to be a national gain, the ultimate consumer must not be the only participant in the advantages of the cheapness so obtained. It is only an advantage when it is shared and enjoyed by the classes interested in production and industry. No doubt foreign nations were wise enough to perceive this in the matter of British supremacy in recent years, and so they increased their tariffs upon our exports, in order to deprive us as a nation of this benefit due to our cheaper production, and it was only in neutral markets where there was any such competitive advantage left us.

The success of the protectionist policy of our foreign competitors, however, in building up their manufacturing industries, in the face of our competition, to an equality with ourselves, has now deprived us of even this last advantage in the matter of such cheapness, as both Germany and France, and the United States are in a position to dispute the possession of every market in the world with us, notwithstanding all that has been said in favour of our Free Trade policy.

A house cannot stand without firm foundations. John Bull's industrial house must have a firm base; that base consists of a prosperous agriculture—employment on the land, and full, varied, and profitable employment in flourishing manufactories, resulting in a prosperous home trade and domestic exchanges.

Here is the prescription to impart vigour to John Bull's constitution.

The British market should be for British labour, and not available for an indefinite amount of foreign labour; the sooner our good market is secured by suitable import duties, the better it will be for British labour and the whole community.

Why be so squeamish about taxing foreign competing labour products while an enormous burden of taxation is heaped upon home production?

CHAPTER XIII.

THE STRUGGLE FOR WAGES AND HIGHER WAGES. A "LIVING WAGE"—A "MINIMUM WAGE."

A Fierce Struggle of who shall descend first to the Lowest Level—The Industrial Clouds are gathering and getting darker every Day—Coal Miners presuming to have a Voice in fixing the Price of Coal—The Circumstances under which the Coal-mining Population discard the Doctrines of Political Economy—A Fine How d'ye do—Can an Irreducible Minimum of a "Living Wage" be fixed?—Partial Protection impossible—Labour "Leaders"—The "Live and let live" Principle—Low Wages, or no Wages at all, will threaten the very Existence of the Nation.

IT goes without saying that with an industrial community like England, prosperity comes with full employment at a good rate of wages.

Society is so constituted that nearly four-fifths of our people have, of necessity, to labour for a livelihood, therefore it is of the utmost importance that the great productive industries of our country should be preserved in a sound state. No one can doubt the seriousness of the question of industrial employment.

If we would have a contented, law-abiding people, there must be employment for them at fair wages, as involuntary idleness brings in its train social degradation, loss of moral fibre, distress, discontent, and, finally, revolution. In this country the wages of labourers and artisans have been higher than the wages paid to continental workers, resulting in a higher, more expensive standard of living in comparison with other European countries.

Of course, custom, climate, artificial regulations, the enjoyment of political liberties, and other matters, will have much to do in fixing the rate of wages, and we are aware how low is the remuneration of labour in Asiatic and semi-barbarous countries. The Hindoo in a Bombay cotton-mill is content with circumstances which would not be tolerated by Oldham operatives.

How will English workers, in the presence of unlimited, unrestricted competition of foreigners, worse lodged, worse clothed, worse fed than themselves, successfully compete with them? This is a question for the upholders of free imports to answer. Will the Englishman enter upon this fierce struggle of who shall descend first to the lowest level? Not when he knows it. Why should he? No wonder there is a labour crusade in this country; it is the inevitable sequel to unrestrained foreign competition. Whatever Socialists in our midst may say or do, the *first step* towards ameliorating the condition of our working classes is security against the competition of those living under lower conditions of life. Foreign competition means a grinding down of the wages of the people, and our poor sink deeper and deeper.

The modern Free Trade economist may well sit down in despair at the prospect before us; he knows the industrial clouds are gathering and getting darker every day. He knows there is abroad a general revolt against the principles and doctrines of his system; he knows the sacred right of "buying in the cheapest

market" is being called into question. The sanctity
of this maxim has vanished into thin air ; there is no
mistake about the current of public opinion—with the
demand of a living wage coupled with a minimum
wage. As these lines are being written, the Miners'
Conciliation Board is sitting deliberating over the
price of coal and a minimum wage ; it is impossible,
at this moment, to estimate what the controversy will
ultimately lead to.

Economic minds will be shocked at the audacity of
coal miners presuming to have a voice in fixing the
price of coal. Grant this position, and the theory
must be applied all round, and then the farm labourer
will regulate the price of wheat, and a similar
rule obtain in all other departments of production.

Let us examine the circumstances under which the
coal-mining population discard the doctrines of
political economy. First of all, the question of
supply and demand. Some twenty years ago the
demand for coal caused high prices, with big wages
for miners ; then the demand for coal was abnormal
—owing to the state of our manufactures, and the
general prosperity of our various industries. This gave
coal-miners a large share of the value of the produce
of their labour. They demanded high wages, and
the *then* circumstances warranted the demand. Coal
being the raw material of the motive power applied,
and being more and more extensively applied to the
transport and manufacturing agencies of the world,
Great Britain—the would-be workshop of the world—
with mines connected at short distances with her

seaports, became the coal depôt of the competing manufactures on the sea-board of foreign States.

Now, however, that these States have settled down to competition, self-protected, and equipped with every tool and advantage of which Great Britain then had a monopoly, the relations of the supply to the demand for coal, etc., are entirely and permanently altered. The British manufacturer, consuming coal in given proportions to every ton of iron and steel, glass-ware, paper, textile and other fabrics, cannot afford to give more for his coal than his foreign competitor gets coal at, and the supply of coal available in relation to the normal demand renders it utterly impossible to maintain rates which, at the wages formerly current, would allow a profit to capital in the winning of coal in Great Britain.

Economic pressure is inexorably pressing down the miner to a poverty and a servitude quite as severe and hopeless as that of the rural and agricultural labourer, for whom the miner has had but scant sympathy.

In these circumstances, the mining population of this country discard the doctrines of political economy which they founded upon in more promising and entirely different circumstances. It has a sort of "heads I win, tails you lose" look about it.

But there it is. When demand pulls on supply and prices rise, the miners' wage is to be regulated by (*i.e.*, to rise with) prices.

When supply pulls on demand, and prices fall, then prices have—is it possible under competition?—to be regulated by wages. Here is a fine how d'ye do. How will it work under conditions which the miner has hitherto upheld and approved? Can an irreducible minimum of a living wage be fixed, not only for miners, but for all other workers in all other employments whatsoever? It would follow, if this were possible, that prices would then be regulated by wages.

But an irreducible minimum for the price of labour would involve an irreducible minimum, determined by it, for the products and the tools of labour. A bottom price for wheat and flour, and for paper, aye, even for share and banking capital, would be as certainly a part of the system as a bottom wage for the miner and a bottom price for coal.

What did the miner say to the extermination of the British agriculturist and the British flour miller? He simply filled his " Co-op " with the products from abroad which could be carried and procured the cheapest, and cared not two straws for the living wage of anybody.

If ever the doctrines of humanity are to effect the political economy of nations, then the principles of Protection and not of Free Trade must be adopted and adhered to. Does the miner, and do the Trade Unions dream of that? They demand partial protection, which is impossible ; the protection of what they individually sell, but competition to the fullest in everything they buy. Every other body, if not so fully demanding the former, has also demanded the latter, and, as the miner, and not Hodge, is this time the victim, the miner shifts his ground and demands a living wage.

The whole thing is a great, a painful, and a necessary object lesson.

We see quite clearly that the available supply and
congestion of labour engaged in our coal-mines, docks,
and railways, is due to the previous degradation and
exploitation of British agriculture ; this super-abund-
ant supply of labour so much exceeds the natural
demand, that restrictive artifices and violent disturbances have resulted.

However, the real state of things is dawning,
although slowly, upon the imaginations of the working classes of England, and when they clearly
understand how they have (under free competing
imports) made themselves the cat's-paw of the
foreigner, without doubt they will run to extremes in
demanding protection for their labour.

We cannot take up a newspaper without reading
of some labour leader advocating the doctrine " that
the rate of wages regulates the price of the article."
It remains to be seen how these leaders will eventually treat the system which upholds cheapness as the
summum bonum of industrial life. It cannot be too
often repeated, that cheap goods spell cheap labour ;
for when goods of any kind are bought, it is really
human labour that is bought; it is labour which gives
commodities their price.

Men on strike against starvation wages do not care
very much for economic laws and dogmas; "sweated"
labourers declare against capital bearing upon their
helplessness ; an excess in the supply of labour
diminishes wages, and when in the toils of the grind-
ing-down process, the law of supply and demand can
have no charm for them. Humanity rises up against
the brutal system of universal unrestricted competi-

tion, and stipulates for the live and let live principle
—fair conditions of production and fair wages.

This infers a standard of living suitable for the
conditions of English work and life. The foreign
standard is one to which they cannot be expected to
bow down.

Universal competition is a struggle between the
working classes of all nations which shall descend first and nearest to the condition of the
brutes. This may be the economical standard
and ethics of Free Trade, but the moral sense
of mankind revolts at the contemplation of it.
Christianity and modern civilisation protest against
it. Slavery (the traffic of God's image carved in
ebony) was found to need legal interference—so is
it to-day as regards the labour question, and unrestricted, universal competition.

Trade Unions are useful in mitigating the sufferings of flesh and blood; artificial regulations are
necessary to prevent excessive competition (which
cannot cure itself) either between employers or
labourers. Why denounce the protective principle?
for without it our industrial building is only resting
on shifting sand. However, those who are responsible
for directing Trade Unionism should always keep in
mind that an undue pressure upon capital may destroy
industry; but, on the other hand, let English statesmen be fully conscious that low wages, or no wages
at all, will threaten the very existence of the nation.

CHAPTER XIV.

PROTECTION TO BRITISH AND IRISH LABOUR.

The Schoolmaster—The Craven Fear of acknowledging a Great Mistake—Solved by the Logic of Facts—The Pretensions of the Medes and Persians—The Growth of Protective Legislation during Recent Years—It is the Work of Statesmen to establish Feasibility of Protection in Practice—·A Wise National Protection—A Policy of Insurance ; a Premium paid for the Purpose of Insuring Domestic Industry—An Infatuated Donkey—Tables (up to date) showing the Certain Annihilation of Our Home Industries.

IN my last chapter I have considered unrestricted imports as bearing down English labour to the level of the worst paid labourers in the world. The time was when our public men talked of the advantages of competition, and blessed " the keen edge of foreign competition." We asked for universal competition, and now we are getting it: our coasts are studded with ports, and so this country is more liable to industrial invasion than any other country in the world. In former times, England's insular position secured for her a large measure of *natural* protection; the cost of carriage and transport and freight preserved our markets from the competition of foreign labour.

The improved ocean transport of recent years has completely changed the aspect of affairs, for the steamship places, with almost the precision of the railway train, the products of foreign labour right into the centres of vast consuming populations, and we are having, to all intents and purposes, *an industrial invasion.*

In every country, excepting England, the loss of natural protection is compensated with artificial protection : foreign countries act upon the instinct of self-preservation. Industrial depression, such as we are at present experiencing, must direct the working people of this country into the paths of common sense, and awaken their instinct of self-preservation : the suffering they are now enduring is but a schoolmaster to educate them out of the power of Free Trade delusions.

" Woe to those who add competition to competition till there is no place left for the worker." Yes, woe to that political economy—or slavery—which forces our workers to live the worst to produce the cheapest. Internal competition is quite enough to consider without the fierce struggle of universal competition, and it will tax all the resources of our rulers to satisfy the claims of labour, according to the conditions of labour in this country, without attempting to regulate affairs subject to universal and unrestricted competition.

The time has arrived for wise National Protection, the protection of British labour in its own market against the products of foreign labour. Why should there be any hesitation or fear in discussing Protection ? Because of the craven fear of acknowledging that you have made a mistake ; to admit that cherished theories, tested by the book of experience, are rebuked and exposed, is painful and humiliating.

The doctrines of Free Trade were supposed to come from certain good men favoured with sudden and preternatural illuminations, and the doctrines, for a time, fascinated the people ; however, the enthusiasm has evaporated, many have been undeceived by bitter experience, and to-day there are scoffers in the land. The tide is on the turn ; for the situation is so transparent that it is obvious that before long the sweeping brush will be applied to our chaotic fiscal arrangements, and root and branch they will be cleared away ; the *laissez-faire* philosophy—a mere phase of opinion—must pass away in the face of the dangers— national and industrial—which press upon us on every side.   Thoughtful men are fast coming to the conclusion that the ideal of Cobden is a miserable failure, and that the millennial vine—planted under the influence of cosmopolitan sentiment—instead of bearing sweet and luscious fruit, has brought forth sour grapes, and they do not exactly see why they, and their children, should always have their teeth on edge.

Many writers in the public press apply the quality of mercy to Free Trade, and look upon the system as a gospel or a revelation from on high.   They forget that applied truth must always be relative, and subject to a great extent to the conditions under which it has to be applied.   Free imports in a free import world might be wisdom—(which the writer does not admit) when populations dwelt in universal peace,

when nation vied with nation in offices of kindness for
the common good of mankind—but free imports in a
Protectionist world are, well, a very different matter.
There is reason to doubt if the men who agitated for
Free Trade indulged in the cry of the cheap loaf from
their bowels of compassion with the sufferings of the
people.   The cheap loaf cry can be interpreted as
euphemistic of cheap labour, which was considered
all important to maintain our manufacturing supremacy.

Free Trade has not a particle of the quality of
mercy pertaining to it.

The pride of the human heart is very great; men
do not like to admit their errors, and turn their backs
upon themselves, particularly when they have posed as
benefactors to their fellow-countrymen.   No, when
people are placed (metaphorically speaking) upon
pedestals, they will not step down gracefully of their
own accord; they will only come down when pushed
over.

We cannot sit quietly under the tattered and worn-
out Free Trade umbrella (labelled free imports), and
think it of any use to shield us from the industrial
storm.   We cannot live on Free Trade traditions; it
is our duty to regard the actual circumstances in
which we are placed at the close of the nineteenth
century.

No doubt "the fat is in the fire" when we speak
of returning to Protection; we are scolded as re-
actionists, and told that England's fiscal policy is
indissoluble, i.e., that it can never be violated, and is
binding upon us for ever.   Some people argue that

because great political measures, passed during this
century, are plainly irrevocable, therefore a commercial measure, passed forty-eight years ago, during
an outburst of optimism, must necessarily be irrevocable also.   Political measures, great changes of
Government, have not been peculiar to this country.
Take, for instance, the lowering of the elective
franchise and Catholic emancipation ; the establishment of religious liberty; Parliamentary reform,
admitting the people to a voice in the management
of national affairs.   These great changes have taken
place in continental countries and in America, but
we do not find these countries following our system
of unrestricted imports.   Legislatures have been
popularised, but no one can say that, outside of
England, commercial legislation has tended in the
direction of free exchanges.   Purely political measures have become inevitable.   Time will tell if all
the changes will tend towards good government and
the security of the State.   The next, or succeeding,
generations will know.

As to commercial or trade policy, in these days of
railways, ocean transport, steam, and electricity, we
have not to wait long to prove the results of commercial policy and fiscal regulations.   Experience,
year by year, and from day to day, has withdrawn
many questions of commercial policy from the domain
of conjecture—solved by the logic of facts.

Looking back upon our history as a great producing
and commercial nation, we find our fiscal regulations
changing with altered circumstances.   It is only
when we come to the sages of 1846 that the preten-

sions of the Medes and Persians are put forth. Then
everything pertaining to national production and
national trade became irrevocably fixed, that is to
say, Free Trade became stereotyped. Industrial and
commercial affairs have changed in the past, and will
change in time to come.

When will the change to Protection on the part of
Great Britain as a national policy come? It will
come after much industrial suffering—the mischief of
unbridled foreign competition in our markets; after
industrial capital has been transferred to foreign
countries; it will come when the conditions of
English labour—be it in the fields, the factory, or the
forge—are unbearable.

We must remember that the people of industrial
England now have votes; are they likely to vote for
unrestricted universal competition? No, but rather
follow their fellow-workers on the Continent and in
America and in British colonies, by heartily embrac-
ing the salvation of Protection. Recent legislation
very clearly indicates that we have left behind us the
Liberal Free Trade philosophy, that the business of
Government was to let things "find their level
naturally"; this doctrine was fashionable some thirty
years ago, but it has fallen into discredit. To-day
all sorts of social experiments are tried, public
opinion has undergone a change, and the Government is called upon to actively interfere in many
directions, witness the special legislation for Ireland,
factory and mines Acts (regulating the employment of
women and children), Acts *re* the importation of
cattle, adulteration Acts, Poor Law, Merchandise

Marks Act, and in many ways protective legislation
has taken place on behalf of the public.

The interposition of Government really means
action being taken for the general benefit, and such
interference is, in principle, united with a protective
system. Why? Because by law men should be
treated fairly—not as mere machines. Go a step in
advance, and you get protection for British labour
against unrestricted foreign competition—the displacement of native labour by the introduction of
cheaper foreign labour. Protection, so far as it is
feasible, of our well-paid, prosperous labour from the
competition of poorly-paid, semi-barbarous labour.
It is the work of statesmen to establish feasibility of
protection in practice. A wise national Protection
will accomplish the following :—It will induce capital
to remain at home for the support of domestic industries by rendering it possible for those industries
to attract its co-operation. It will foster and multiply
native industries, to support the national growth in
comfort, population and power. It will do all this—
and more—for it will secure the power of bargaining
and of influencing foreign markets in our favour.

We want import duties in scope and amount
sufficient to protect native labour and native industries, and secure legitimate cheapness. Protection
of this kind may be viewed as in the nature of a
policy of insurance, and the duties levied on competing imports as a premium paid for the purpose of
insuring domestic industry, which is the mainstay
and back-bone of the nation, against risk and disaster. Where could a system of insurance be applied

to a purpose more necessary, wise, and important ?
John Bull insures all sorts of things.   Let us hope that
he will soon—very soon—take out a policy of insurance on behalf of British and Irish labour, and
British and Irish industries.

Should he fail in so doing, he will prove himself to
be—well—an infatuated donkey !

The following tables compiled by Mr. Sibson S.
Rigg, Manchester, from official sources, will give the
reader some idea of the artificially stimulated competition (external competition added to internal
competition) forced upon British workers, and showing the *certain annihilation of our home industries.*

GREAT INCREASE OF AGRICULTURAL IMPORTS.

	Quantities.	Values.		
	1892.	1855.	1886.	1892.
		£	£	£
Cows, Oxen, &c., No........	502,237 ...	1,333,763 ...	5,068,846 ...	9,224,011
Sheep, No......	79,048 ...	282,844 ...	2,010,194 ...	125,659
Swine, No.	3,826 ...	— ...	63,357 ...	12,465
Horses, No.....	20,994 ...	— ...	189,901 ...	425,401
Bacon & Hams, cwt............	5,134,510 ...	617,423 ...	8,402,828 ...	10,893,833
Beef, cwts.....	2,355,031 ...	482,802 ...	2,178,677 ...	4,801,736
Butter, cwts...	2,183,009 ...	2,449,522 ...	8,141,438 ...	11,965,190
M'rine, cwts...	1,305,350 ...	inc.w.but ...	2,962,264 ...	3,712,884
Cheese, cwts..	2,232,817 ...	1,027,774 ...	3,871,359 ...	5,416,784
Eggs, 1000's..	1,336,730 ...	236,865 ...	2,884,063 ...	3,794,718
Poultry and Rabbits.....	— ...	— ...	639,704 ...	886,692
Hops, cwts....	187,507 ...	171,955 ...	447,253 ...	960,280
Lard, cwts....	1,239,051 ...	310,036 ...	1,544,632 ...	2,233,011
Pork, cwts.....	360,461 ...	489,935 ...	631,538 ...	616,427

GREAT INCREASE OF AGRICULTURAL IMPORTS—*Contd.*

	Quantities.		Values.	
	1892.	1855. £	1886. £	1892. £
Maize, cwts...	35,381,224 ...	2,640,250 ...	7,617,470 ...	9,425,211
Potatoes, cwts.	3,008,336 ...	10,196 ...	799,265 ...	950,332
Tallow, cwts..	1,375,679 ...	2,647,173 ...	1,299,214 ...	1,747,968
Meat, salted, &c., cwts...	950,074 ...	— ...	1,281,245 ...	2,296,710
Mutton, fresh, cwts.	1,699,966 ...	— ...	1,405,383 ...	3,447,102
Milk, con., cts.	481,374 ...	— ...	— ...	930,288
Onions, bush.	4,420,276 ...	— ...	506,710 ...	724,040
Vegetables....	— ...	— ...	540,670 ...	1,016,280

Total........   —   £12,700,538 £52,486,011 £75,607,022
1892 over 1886, increase 44·0 per cent.

£   £   £
Flour, cwts....22,106,009 ... 2,304,106 ... 8,228,051 ... 12,267,453
Increase 47·8 per cent.

This large import of flour instead of grain deprives British millers of wages, and also deprives our breeders and feeders of stock of a vast mass of manufactured food useful in the production of *Meat, Milk, Butter,* and *Cheese.*

Corn, excl. of   cwts.   £   £   £
maize & flour 103,429,894...13,644,544 ... 27,702,658...37,041,428

—   £28,649,188 £88,416,720 £124,915,903
Increase 33·6 per cent.
Population ....36,312,715 ... 38,104,973
Increase 5·0 per cent.

From this table it will be seen that with an increased population, 1892 over 1886 of only 5 per cent., we have at the same time an increase of agricultural imports, apart from corn, 44·0 per cent., flour

47·8 per cent., and wheat, oats, and barley 33·6 per cent., together in value some £36,500,000 of an increase.

GREAT INCREASE OF MANUFACTURED IMPORTS.

	1886.	1892.
	£	£
Watches and Clocks	1,092,977	1,204,188
Gloves and Boots	1,855,606	2,342,911
Leather dressed, &c.	5,536,225	6,397,821
Paper	1,526,221	2,412,001
Books, Prints, Stationery, Pictures	978,830	1,149,853
Glass	1,544,612	2,434,450
Paint colours	778,027	1,013,480
Skins, Furs, and Rugs	1,325,315	1,714,345
Furniture, Housefittings, &c.	948,240	1,176,351
Toys	618,376	807,103
Matches	417,644	367,654
Wood sawn, &c.	9,145,171	12,313,674
Chemicals	1,284,537	1,502,294
China, Porcelain, &c.	521,418	656,884
Arms	603,657	244,872
Lace	1,310,639	966,634
Musical Instruments	729,805	997,016
Cordage	506,781	585,043
Embroidery	194,046	483,014
Straw plaiting	572,687	586,325
Stones cut, &c.	549,064	703,345
Caoutchouc manufacture	353,729	408,150
Cork manufacture	443,022	608,989
Oil Perfumed and Perfumery	293,915	377,694
Artificial Flowers	272,435	328,624
Buttons and Beads	463,031	409,054
Hats	179,525	170,741
Hair manufacture	99,743	133,090
Sundries	656,764	749,204
	£34,802,042	£43,244,804

1892 over 1886, increase 24·3 per cent.

Textiles.	1855. £	1886. £	1892. £
Cotton yarn and cloth...	359,300 ...	2,308,957 ...	3,286,787
Silk do. do. ...	3,051,865 ...	10,920,516 ...	11,853,577
Woollen do. do. ...	946,988 ...	10,564,721 ...	11,765,829
Linen do. do. ...	— ...	807,814 ...	1,172,511
Jute do. do. ...	— ...	124,638 ...	51,939
	£4,358,153	£24,726,646	£28,130,643

1892 over 1886, increase 13·8 per cent.

Totals.....................£59,528,888...£71,375,445

Increase, 20·0 per cent.

GREAT INCREASE OF METAL IMPORT.

	1855. £	1886. £	1892. £
Iron ore......................	— ...	1,894,626 ...	2,716,820
Pig iron......................	— ...	221,378 ...	235,681
Bar, &c.	542,401 ...	957,057 ...	692,259
Old Iron	— ...	31,873 ...	41,094
Steel, unwrought...........	— ...	112,342 ...	62,486
Iron and steel manuf.......	14,493 ...	2,200,265 ...	2,532,118
Iron girders, &c.............	— ...	— ...	502,574
Sewing Machines...........	— ...	258,740 ...	255,255
Copper ore regulus—......	1,433,693 ...	2,116,615 ...	3,877,479
Wrought and unwrought copper......................	975,196 ...	1,884,301 ...	1,714,698
Copper manufacture.......	— ...	— ...	45,325
Lead ore......................	— ...	135,464 ...	80,812
Lead, pig or sheet....... ..	161,828 ...	1,373,302 ...	1,976,436
Lead manufacture..........	— ...	— ...	6,690
Tin ore......................	— ...	25,633 ...	133,181
Ditto Blocks..............	190,257 ...	2,318,070 ...	2,743,814
Ditto manufactures.....	— ...	4,126 ...	6,860
Silver ore....................	564,580 ...	1,030,488 ...	3,032,169
Zinc ore......................	— ...	62,723 ...	166,378
Ditto crude in cakes....	314,267 ...	774,938 ...	1,102,591
Ditto manufactures......	130,441 ...	326,004 ...	463,080
Other metals wrought.....	— ...	339,970 ...	284,317
Total...................	£4,327,156	£16,067,915	£22,672,117

1892 over 1886, increase 41·9 per cent.

From the above it will be seen that with an increase of population of 5 per cent. in 1892 over 1886, we have at the same time an increased import of various manufactures 24·3 per cent., textile manufactures 13·8 per cent., while our metal import shows the enormous increase of 41·9 per cent.   It may be considered by some to be an advantage to receive all these labour products from foreign countries, but surely the un-employed should be considered in the matter, whose only capital is their labour.   Strikes we have in plenty, but what we want is a strike of both masters and men against the injustice of competing imports being admitted free.

STATISTICS REFERRING TO 1893.
Agriculture and free imports.

Board of Trade Returns of our agricultural imports for last year, 1893, compared with 1886 and also with 1855 :

	Quantities.	Values.		
	1893.	1855. £	1886. £	1893. £
Cows, Oxen, &c...No.	340,045	1,333,763	5,068,846	6,262,861
Sheep..............No.	62,682	282,844	2,010,194	88,530
Swine..............No.	138	—	63,357	413
Horses.............No.	22,431	—	189,901	594,214
Bacon & Hams.Cwts.	4,187,298	617,423	8,402,828	11,370,067
Beef..............Cwts.	2,008,565	482,802	2,178,677	4,109,593
Butter............Cwts.	2,327,474	2,449,523	8,141,438	12,753,593
Margarine........Cwts.	1,299,970	in.w.but.	2,962,264	3,655,344
Cheese...........Cwts.	2,077,739	1,027,774	3,871,359	5,161,460
Eggs.............100's	11,045,986	236,865	2,884,063	3,875,647
Poultry and Rabbits..	—	—	639,704	866,696
Pork....................	—	—	631,538	745,121
Meat, salted, &c.Cwts.	768,309	—	1,281,245	1,945,123
Mutton, fresh....Cwts.	1,971,500	—	1,405,383	3,873,863
Lard.............Cwts.	1,201,860	310,036	1,544,632	2,978,639

STATISTICS REFERRING TO 1893—*Continued.*

	Quantities.	Values.		
	1893.	1855.	1886.	1893.
		£	£	£
Tallow............Cwts.	1,539,397	2,647,173	1,299,214	2,161,407
Hops..............Cwts	204,392	171,955	447,253	1,141,294
Potatoes...........Cwts.	2,828,125	10,196	799,265	906,952
Onions......... Bushels	4,671,809	—	506,710	783,405
Vegetables..............	—	—	540,670	1,076,749
Hay.................Tons	263,050	—	—	1,382,812
Straw (not for hats) Tons	27,337	—	—	73,046
Moss Litter......Tons	93,426	—	—	116,098
Maize.............Cwts.	32,908,503	2,640,250	7,617,470	7,892,629
Clover & Grass Seeds Cwts.	333,412	—	589,786	792,061
Garden Seeds....Lbs.	3,664,601	—	42,796	101,523
Plants, Shrubs, &c....	—	—	262,961	313,482
Farinaceous subst.....	—	—	809,855	1,297,113
Milk, conde'sed,Cwts.	501,005	—	—	1,009,755
Guano, &c........Tons	552,561	3,547,007	1,475,737	1,823,687
Apples.........Bushels	3,459,984	55,048	857,095	843,532
Pears, Cherries, and Plums.......Bushels	2,038,502	—	—	873,395
Nuts as fruit...........	—	—	457,066	522,962
Cider...................	—	—	—	23,814

£15,812,659 £56,981,307 £81,416,880

1893 over 1886, increase 42·8 per cent.

Flour..............Value   £2,304,106 £8,228,051 £9,761,510
Flour, quantity..Cwts.   1,904,224 14,689,560 20,408,168
Increase value 18·6 per cent., increase quantity 38·7 per cent.
Corn, excl've of maize
  and wheat flour.....   £13,644,544 £27,702,658 £33,526,232
Increase value, 20·9 per cent.

Total..............   £31,761,309 £92,912,016 £124,704,632
1893 over 1886, increase 35·3 per cent.
Population..............   27,821,730 36,312,715 38,429,992
1893 over 1886, increase 5·7 per cent.

GREAT INCREASE OF MANUFACTURED IMPORTS.

	1886.	1893.
	£	£
Watches and clocks	1,092,977 ...	1,161,697
Gloves and boots	1,855,606 ...	2,495,495
Leather dressed, &c.	5,536,225 ...	6,581,142
Leather manufactured un-enumerated	167,480 ...	289,075
Paper	1,526,221 ...	2,347,080
Books, prints, stationery, and pictures	978,830 ...	1,197,523
Glass	1,544,612 ...	2,443,259
Painters' colours	778,027 ...	991,329
Skins, furs, and rugs	1,325,315 ...	1,763,837
House frames, fittings, &c.	545,306 ...	660,315
Furniture	810,497 ...	1,262,816
Toys	618,376 ...	884,235
Matches	417,644 ...	362,560
Wood sawn, &c.	9,145,171 ...	14,314,685
Chemicals	1,284,537 ...	1,355,646
China, porcelain, &c.	521,418 ...	625,532
Arms	603,667 ...	216,100
Lace	1,310,639 ...	1,032,127
Musical instruments	729,805 ...	923,920
Cordage	506,781 ...	502,145
Embroidery	194,046 ...	494,768
Straw plaiting	572,687 ...	668,674
Stones cut, &c.	549,064 ...	733,614
Caoutchouc manufactures	353,729 ...	375,487
Cork manufactures	433,022 ...	605,521
Oil perfumed and perfumery	293,915 ...	410,546
Artificial flowers	272,435 ...	336,330
Buttons and beads	463,031 ...	339,957
Hats	179,525 ...	166,405
Pickles, vinegar, and sauce	169,118 ...	161,764
Miscellaneous	494,915 ...	644,228
	£35,284,610	£46,337,812

Increase, 1893 over 1886, 3·1 per cent.

Import of sugar, refined, £10,599,331 from the Continent.

Textiles.	1855. £	1886. £	1893. £
Cotton yarn and cloth ...	359,300 ...	2,308,957 ...	3,043,022
Silk ,, ,, ...	3,051,865 ...	10,920,516 ...	12,026,616
Woollen ,, ,, ...	946,988 ...	10,564,721 ...	12,081,754
Goats' wool yarn ,, ...	— ...	97,458 ...	138,354
Linen ,, ,, ...	— ...	807,814 ...	1,103,377
Jute ,, ,, ...	— ...	124,638 ...	49,724

£4,358,153   £24,824,104   £28,442,847

Increase, 1893 over 1886, 14·5 per cent.

Totals.........................£60,108,714   £74,791,660

Increase, 1893 over 1886, 24·4 per cent.

GREAT INCREASE OF METAL IMPORT.

	1855. £	1886. £	1893. £
Iron ore............................	—	... 1,894,626 ...	2,792,028
Pig iron............................	—	... 221,378 ...	174,038
Bar iron	542,401 ...	957,057 ...	593,083
Old iron, &c......................	—	... 31,873 ...	34,554
Steel, unwrought................	—	... 112,342 ...	90,506
Iron and steel manufactures	14,493 ...	2,200,265 ...	2,545,639
Iron girders, &c................	—	... — ...	419,383
Sewing machines...............	—	... 258,740 ...	225,241
Copper ore.......................	1,433,693 ...	2,116,615 ...	3,318,962
,, wrought and unwr't	975,196 ...	1,884,301 ...	1,975,865
,, manufactured	—	... — ...	72,719
Lead ore..........................	—	... 135,464 ...	49,967
,, pig or sheet..............	161,828 ...	1,373,302 ...	1,855,215
,, manufacture.............	—	... — ...	5,840
Tin ore............................	—	... 25,633 ...	119,890
,, blocks......................	190,257 ...	2,318,070 ...	2,892,107
,, manufactures.............	—	... 4,126 ...	12,569
Silver ore........................	564,580 ...	1,030,488 ...	3,069,131
Zinc ore..........................	—	... 62,723 ...	171,201
,, crude, in cakes..........	314,267 ...	774,938 ...	1,007,397
,, manufactures.............	130,441 ...	326,004 ...	398,363
Other metal, wrought, not enumerated..................	—	... 339,970 ...	301,953

£4,327,156   £16,067,915   £22,125,591

1893 over 1886, 38·1 per cent.

From the above it will be seen that, with an increase of population of 5·7 per cent. in 1893 over 1886, we have at the same time an increased import of various manufactures 31·1 per cent., textile manufactures 24·4 per cent., while our metal import shows 38·1 per cent.

These tables prove conclusively that Protectionist countries undersell us in the British home market.

CHAPTER XV.

As a nation we have done a large and thriving export trade. Some people argue that this is owing to
Free Trade, but long before the advent of free imports our foreign trade steadily augmented; as a
fact the protective system created in England all the
elements necessary for the prosecution of a foreign
trade; we had domestic activity and industry, a
flourishing agriculture and prosperous manufactures;
—the means of purchase were immense; the sure
home market created the means of purchase; thus we
possessed what was indispensable for foreign trade—
productions for export.

At this prosperous period of our history we required

fresh markets, markets to still further increase the means of purchase for a rapidly growing population. At this juncture, under the scare of scarcity and high-priced food, we adopted the adventurous policy of throwing our markets open to the world; we did not wait to see if the supplies of food could be obtained from the growers of grain on land within the territories of the British Crown.

In the rapid growth of manufactures, and with a practical monopoly of important industries, it was considered necessary to obtain food at the lowest price to prosecute the export trade, which trade the country was to depend upon for the support of the population. To manufacture for the world cheap production was essential, and, to this end, food must be cheapened, the workers must be fed with *untaxed foreign* supplies, no matter how home-grown food was taxed. So argued the Free Traders of 1846.

The experiment has been tried, and we find that it involved the diversion of home labour from agricultural pursuits, and the consequent loss of domestic exchanges.

The general result of the adventurous policy is apparent in the sacrifice of our original sources of income, and in the gradual loss of the export trade; thus the wealth of the country is lessened.

If Free Trade had been a success the reverse would have been the case. We should have seen new industries spring into existence, new sources of livelihood established, and the export trade increasing in proportion to the increase of population.

When John Bull was enthralled with the folly of

Free Trade he acted like a reckless gambler, and risked his ample fortune on the chance of an exceptional result; he disturbed the normal growth of his home industries and foreign trade by adopting the artificial remedies—political baubles—of his Free Trade advisers.

The manufacturing interests — headed by King Cotton—clamoured for Free Trade and the cheap loaf; the owners of mills and factories, stimulated by selfishness, decreed a sentence of death to British agriculture and agricultural labourers. We have witnessed the downward course of British agriculture; we now witness the collapse of British manufactures. Our position is replete with dangers; foreign corn displaced home-grown corn, and foreign manufactures are fast displacing British manufactures. It is the story of the quack killed by his own nostrums. We have seen what the decline of agriculture is to agricultural labourers; we shall now behold what is the result of the decline of British manufactures upon the operative classes of our country. Truly, " Time tries all things."

The advocates of Free Trade led their converts to believe that high wages would result from their system. The cheapening of commodities, by opening the home markets, doubtless gave an increased purchasing power of the wages *then* earned; but instead of raising the nominal value of the sum earned, the operation of free competing imports tended to reduce it.

Free Trade can cheapen commodities, but it cannot raise wages. If a protective policy had been pursued, foreign markets would have been influenced, and wages maintained or raised.   Under Free Trade we are powerless to open foreign markets.   Before Free Trade we *commanded* foreign markets; but when our own markets were thrown open, it advantaged the foreign competitor, and imposed upon the native producer an artificially stimulated competition.   Any advance in the rate of wages in this country is due to the action of Trade Unionism; nothing is more absurd than to attribute it to unrestricted universal competition.

There is a difference between the Free Trade of Mr. Cobden and the Free Trade of Mr. John Bright. The former looked for his system to be established on an international basis, although he did not count the difference of wages.   Mr. Bright insisted upon the right of free buying, and disregarded the free selling; with him reciprocity was no part of the bargain. Mr. John Bright urged the working men to restrain their longings for an increase in wages, so that we might be able to manufacture at the same prices as foreign competitors.   Mr. Bright considered this indispensable to our success.   His views are very fully expressed in the following extracts from a letter written to a Nottingham gentleman, November 29, 1886 :—

"If your manufacturers are unable to compete with their rivals in other parts of the country or in foreign countries, their business must be unprosperous, and may gradually decay.   If the cause of these be in the high wages claimed and paid in your town, unless wages in other parts can be raised, it would seem to follow that your trade can only be preserved by a reduction of your wages, or by some other diminution of the cost of manufacturing, if such be possible. There have been cases in which trades have been driven from towns and districts by special circumstances, causing an increase of cost in manufacturing and production, and those acquainted with the condition of your town and trade can judge much better than I can. If Trade Unions, for example, insist on wages which a trade cannot pay, the particular trade may, and indeed must, suffer—must become unprosperous, and may decay and be driven to some other district where *labour is free* from the *interference* and *unwise restrictions* of *combinations of workmen*."

Mr. Bright's letter gives a plain issue—either there must be protection against the products of cheap foreign labour in our markets, or British workmen must accept lower wages. That they will not submit to the latter is a certainty. It is a pity Mr. Bright did not live to express his views upon the living wage and an irreducible minimum, and the doctrine that wages must regulate prices. But Mr. Bright is spared a lot of trouble in not witnessing the upset of his life's work.

The ruthless competition of over-plus foreign supply in our markets is removing the scales from the eyes of our working classes. They begin to feel that they are victimised for the sake of a theory.

The common sense of the people, in the face of present circumstances, must declare with irresistible force that Free Trade is unsound as a national and a trade policy. Day by day we are becoming acquainted with the devastating consequences of the let alone system, and common sense must come to the rescue. Yes, common sense will declare that Free Trade was simply an artifice to tide over a political difficulty, and that experience has proved it to have been a colossal blunder.

We are thankful that the common sense of our children in the colonies has saved them from the blunder. They were not to be scared and wheedled into compliance with the behests of a fanciful and fantastic system.

Free Trade commenced its career in this country with an exhibition of national passion or madness; the end of the system will be accompanied with national sadness. Already we feel an uncomfortable gloom. Our political system is out of joint, and our industrial interests show sure signs of decadence; we are experiencing political disturbances and trade despondency; we are conscious that our Free Trade policy has made us the laughing-stock and plaything of Protectionist countries. There is the conviction that we have fallen upon evil days—days of crushing taxation, political babblement, strife, and misunderstanding, days of misery and poverty for vast masses of our people.

It is becoming apparent that Great Britain, in departing from an imperial policy, pursued the wrong course, and no amount of mere political manœuvring will put national affairs in order. Having disregarded national interests, and forsaken the landmarks

of true statesmanship, we stand on a declivity. No
wonder the outlook is perplexing.

In these chapters I have traced the wilful wan-
derings of John Bull into paths of error and disappointment; ruin stares him in the face. I have
shown the downward course of the *laissez-faire* philosophy, how Englishmen have been the victims of
self-destruction; and now they have reached the
edge of the abyss, we must expect to hear a wail of
remorse and reproach.

The wild theories of the Manchester School (the
"Little England" politicians) have made huge gaps
and fissures in the State, which only a great outburst of national sentiment, wisely directed by
statesmanship, can repair; this alone can check
the present radical and revolutionary movement, and
curb the restless vagaries of political charlatans. We
have foreign manufactures pouring into the country,
the products of low wages and long hours, whilst our
working people are fiercely fighting their employers
at the dictation of socialist agitators; the result is
that many of our trades are crippled, and others which
formerly flourished have altogether disappeared, or
are on the point of collapsing. Our work people demand high wages coupled with short hours, and at
the same time stand out for cheap commodities.
How will they be undeceived? When they find out
for themselves that a working population cannot
exist upon cheap foreign foods and goods without
money to buy them. This will end the delusion that
Free Trade benefits the labour of England; it is an
entire perversion of fact to say that the competition

of cheap foreign labour in our markets benefits English labour. The instinct of self-preservation will detect the lie, for this instinct is given to man for good and commendable uses.

Politicians and writers in the public press are always talking of trade depression, but they all give the wrong causes for it. They do not care to admit that Free Trade is a sham, and that under free competing imports British industry can never revive and flourish. The Free Trade politician will not cover himself with odium by frankly admitting that the disgraceful advocacy of one-sided Free Trade has brought the industrial interests of the country into their ruinous condition ; he dreads the complete exposure of his false system, therefore we witness the dreary work of concealment. The true issue of the system is overlaid with other and foreign issues in the hope of distracting public attention, obfuscating the mind of the nation to prevent a clear judgment. Politicians who have orated and stumped Free Trade will have to get rid of their conceit and vanity ere they admit their doctrines to be unreal and corrupt. The uprooting of foul weeds is no easy task.

When the day of awakening has come the cry of the miserable toilers of our swamped industries will be loud enough to stir up the British Lion to make a significant growl—a growl to frighten the Free Trade politicians. When that fearful cry of *Failure* is heard throughout the land, then will follow, and speedily follow, the reversal of Free Trade by a return to Protection. There will probably be a vast

amount of mischief perpetrated before Englishmen
clearly understand how they have been deluded. It
will be from the bitterness of their hearts that the cry
Failure will be uttered ; there will be wide-spread
poverty and misery among the working classes ; our
markets will be crowded out with foreign-made goods,
and there will be a general stoppage of our mills and
factories, forges and furnaces ; in a word, rottenness
in all our industries.

The time of awakening was foretold by Disraeli in
his grave prophecy on the third reading of the Repeal of the Corn Laws Bill :—

" It may be in vain now, in the midnight of their
intoxication, to tell them that there will be an
awakening of bitterness. It may be idle now, in the
spring-tide of their economic frenzy, to warn them
that there will be an ebb of trouble. But the dark
and inevitable hour will arrive ; then—when their
spirit is softened by misfortune—they will recur to
those principles which made England great, and in
our belief can alone keep England great. They may
then, perchance, remember, not with unkindness,
those who, betrayed and deserted, were neither
ashamed nor afraid to struggle for the good old
cause—the cause with which are associated principles
the most popular, sentiments the most entirely
national—the cause of labour, the cause of the people,
the cause of England."

It would appear that the time for the fulfilment of
this prophecy is not far distant, for, on all sides,
chronic discontent stares us in the face ; the question
of industrial employment is shaking our social fabric

to its foundations. We, year in and year out, witness the struggle between capital and labour ; but there is another struggle looming in the distance—the struggle between labour and society. With the latter will come disorder and revolution. It is the duty of all loyal citizens to do all in their power to avert the fearful catastrophe of a *social revolution*. If, at this juncture, the intelligence of the people does not stem the rising radical-socialistic madness, constitutional government will totter to its fall, and be succeeded by a pandemonium. *National ruin can only be averted by the prompt adoption of an Imperial policy.*

No accurate notion of the true position of affairs can be gathered from the attitude of politicians ; ostrich like, they are determined not to see existing facts ; they dare not confess that the logic of events is *compelling* the nation to change its policy. Liberals resist the detection of the action of their pernicious policy, and Tories lack the faculty of estimating the disasters coming upon the nation from the continued operation of free competing imports. Politicians will do anything rather than trace the true source of the prevailing misery of the country ; to do so would overwhelm them with ruin.

Liberals are "reformers," they can reform everything, but they cannot reform their own creations. Tories, or Unionists, as they prefer, to-day, to call themselves, cannot tamper with Free Trade, for it has long been the Mumbo-Jumbo of British politics.

We are all expected to bend and tremble before the authority of Mumbo-Jumbo. Who dare show a spirit of insubordination to its mysterious but stu-

M

pendous authority ?   Who dare risk their reputation
by laughing at the hideous mask, or condemn the
sovereignty and the worship of the politician's
Mumbo-Jumbo?

Nothing must disturb the mystery of the oracle,
for Mumbo-Jumbo is composed of such inflammable
material that a spark would ignite it, and cause a
political conflagration.   However, there are sure signs
that the Free Trade system will soon come to an
ignoble end; the political and social farce will be
played out, and the Mumbo-Jumbo of the platform
and the press will terrorise no more.

CHAPTER XVI.

PROTECTION DOES NOT HINDER AN EXPORT TRADE. PROTECTIONIST COUNTRIES UNDERSELL US IN THE HOME MARKET.

Protection the Immovable Policy of Government—The Great
Exhibition of 1851—Exhibits *created* and *nurtured* by Pro-
tection—What has Industry *un*protected to show?—The
Fiscal Policy of Germany—"Made in Germany"—"Be-
side the Mark"—Statistics of the Growth of Exports—
France, Germany, and the United States—"No European
Nation has prospered as we have"—Internal Production :
Statistics *re* Pig-iron in the United Kingdom, the United
States, and Germany—Steel in the United States,
1880 and 1890; Wool retained for Manufacture in the
United Kingdom, the United States, France, and Ger-
many; Silk Manufacture in the United States and the
United Kingdom—During 1893, Eighty-three Persons out
of every Hundred in the United Kingdom subsisted on
Foreign Wheat—The Downward Movement.

ALL great nations have adopted Protection, and, to-
day, outside of England (among great nations),
Protection continues the universal creed of the people,
and the immovable policy of Government.

England became a great agricultural and manufacturing country under Protection, and enjoyed the
largest foreign trade. The prosperity of a nation
depends upon the cultivation of its soil, and the
creation of manufacturing industries, because two
values and two markets are thereby established, *i.e.*,

179

manufacturing creates a market for food products, and the production of food creates a demand for manufactured goods.

To maintain a proper balance of employment is to ensure comfort and prosperity for the people.

The great object of American statesmanship has been the creation of manufacturing industries ; and this object has been realised by the aid of protective duties, thus finding employment for an enormously increasing population.

The rapid growth of the iron and steel trades in the United States proves the wisdom of American fiscal policy. Home production for home consumption has been the corner-stone of America's industrial system.

We need not look away from our own country ; let our thoughts revert to the Great Exhibition of 1851. How were the great mechanical industries represented at that exhibition brought into existence ? Those exhibits—the marvel of the world—were created and nurtured by Protection.

We can point to the results of Protected industry all the world over, but what has industry *un*protected to show ? Ireland's *un*protected industries are ruined. Turkey and Asia Minor, viewed from an industrial standpoint, present a sad spectacle, mainly caused by the absence of import duties, or low import duties.

Take the case of Germany. With the most stringent protective system has arisen a marvellous development of manufacturing industries, and German agriculture, too, has been progressive. Germany protected herself against the cheaper manufactures of

England. She has no reason to regret the course pursued, for mills, factories, and productive works have been established to support a large population. German production for German consumption has resulted in German production for export, and to-day our markets are crowded out with articles "Made in Germany."

It is all very well for supporters of Free Trade to say, " Every nation adopting high tariffs has virtually removed itself from competition," but the facts are all the other way, because protective nations are competing, not simply in neutral markets, but in the British market at home. To talk of Free Trade giving facilities for cheap purchase, and cheap production, is beside the mark when, in spite of this cheapness, foreign goods are placed in the British market in successful competition with similar goods of home production.

We may argue that, if the cheapness derived from free importation cheapened production in this country, then the products of native labour would keep similar productions out of the British home market. *But it is not so.*

The following statistics demonstrate the growth of exports by Protectionist countries :—

France—Exports (special)	...	...	...	1854	£56,548,000
,,	,,	,,	... ...	1859	90,657,000
,,	,,	,,	... ...	1864	116,978,000
,,	,,	,,	... ...	1866	127,224,000
,,	,,	,,	... ...	1872	150,464,000
,,	,,	,,	... ...	1875	154,904,000
,,	,,	,,	... ...	1882	142,976,000
,,	,,	,,	... ...	1889	148,160,000
,,	,,	,,	... ...	1890	148,805,000

Germany—Exports (special)	...	...	1872	£116,031,000
„ „ „	... ...	...	1876	127,385,000
„ „ „	... ...	...	1878	144,357,000
„ „ „	... ...	...	1881	148,850,000
„ „ „	... ...	...	1883	163,610,000
„ „ „	... ...	...	1888	160,295,000

United States—Exports	...	...	...	1865	£28,524,000
„ „ „	...	...	...	1869	57,326,000
„ „ „	...	...	...	1873	105,215,000
„ „ „	...	...	...	1878	141,814,000
„ „ „	...	...	...	1881	184,151,000
„ „ „	...	...	...	1890	176,102,000

Cobden clubites frequently remark, " No European nation has prospered as we have." Well, in the forty years ending 1880, we increased our foreign trading 453 per cent., Belgium increased hers 917 per cent., Austria, 765 per cent., Russia, 626 per cent., France., 429 per cent., Holland, 382 per cent. Again, take twenty years ending 1880, and we find Great Britain increasing her foreign trade 46 per cent., Russia, 215 per cent., Austria, 144 per cent., Holland, 114 per cent., Belgium, 111 per cent. Therefore, although England forty years ago had such an enormous start of all the world, she has not been keeping her place in the direction of relative advance.

The reader will find a complete record of the exports of British and Irish produce in the table given in Chapter VIII.

Let us pass away from the foreign trading side of the question—which is not the only standard of prosperity—and consider the subject of internal production.

Pig iron produced in the United Kingdom :—

			Million Tons.
1865-9	(Annual average)	...	4·9
1870-4	„	„	...	6·4
1875-9	„	„	...	6·4
1880-4	„	„	...	8·1
1885-9	„	„	...	7·7

Pig iron produced in the United States :—

			Thousands of Tons.
1865-9	(Annual average)	...	1·297
1870-4	„	„	...	2·176
1875-9	„	„	...	2·201
1880-4	„	„	...	4·259
1885-8[1]	„	„	...	5·659

[1] Four years.

Pig iron produced in Germany :—

			Thousands of Tons.
1865-9	(Annual average)	...	1·165
1870-4	„	„	...	1·818
1875-9	„	„	...	2·037
1880-4	„	„	...	3·219
1885-8[1]	„	„	...	3·894

[1] Four years.

As regards the United States, the increase in the production of steel rails and ingots of steel is still more remarkable.

	Year ending May, 1880. (Tons of 2,000 lbs.)	Year ending June, 1890.
Basic steel	—	62,173
Bessemer	985,208	3,788,572
Open-hearth	84,302	504,351
Crucible	76,201	85,536
Clapp-Griffiths ...	—	83,963
Robert Bessemer ...	—	4,504
	1,145,711	4,466,926

Thus, the total increase is 290 per cent., and the production of Bessemer has been quadrupled, and that of open-hearth process is six times as great.

The following tables, *re* the woollen and silk industries, will repay perusal :—

Wool retained for manufacture in the United Kingdom, the United States, France, and Germany respectively, in the years 1866, 1876, and 1884 :—

		1866.	1876.	1884.
		lbs.	lbs.	lbs.
[1]	United Kingdom	313,000,000 ...	369,000,000 ...	381,000,000
[1]	United States ...	229,707,000 ...	235,020,000 ...	376,036,000
[2]	France	190,119,000 ...	271,484,000 ...	356,767,000
[2]	Germany ...	No returns ...	143,260,000 ...	232,962,000

[1] Imported and home grown.
[2] Home grown not included, amount unknown.

Silk manufacture in the United States and the United Kingdom :—

United States :	1860.	1870.	1880.
Value of raw material used (dollar, 4s. 2d.) ...	£ 812,870	£ 1,628,658	£ 3,864,409
United Kingdom : Value of raw material imported, less re-exports	6,482,066	5,774,510	3,383,373
United Kingdom : Silk manufactures imported, less re-exports ...	3,119,395,	15,078,622	13,065,912

Here we observe the simultaneous progress of the silk manufacture in the United States, and decay in this country for twenty years.

Our importation of silk manufactures has quadrupled.

We have conclusive evidence in the statistics included in Chapter XIV. that Protectionist countries are displacing us in the home market, not only with food products, but every variety of manufactured goods,[1] and, moreover, it is impossible to avoid the conclusion that these Protectionist countries have relatively increased their home production for home consumption more than we have. With an ever-increasing importation of food products we witness a progressive decline of agricultural employment for our people, and of the condition and production of British soil. According to Sir John Lawes, " The consumption of the country, with the population corrected up to the middle of this year (1893), will be

[1] In the Report (majority) of the Royal Commission on Depression of Trade and Industry the Commissioners state, Nos. 67 and 76 :—" We are disposed to think that one of the chief agencies which have tended to perpetrate this state of things is the Protectionist policy of so many foreign countries, which has become more marked during the last ten years than at any previous period of similar length. The high prices which Protection secures to the producer within the protected area naturally stimulate production, and impel him to engage in competition in foreign markets. The surplus production which cannot find a market at home is sent abroad, and in foreign markets undersells the commodities produced under less artificial conditions."

Again, "The effect of foreign tariffs and bounties, and the restrictive commercial policy of foreign countries in limiting our markets." (*Why so, if a nation imposing an import duty pays it?*)

Again they say, " Our trade with foreign countries is becoming less profitable in proportion as their markets are becoming more difficult of access, owing to restrictive tariffs ; " and further, " The growing stringency of the commercial policy of these countries tends to make it far less profitable."

29,000,000 quarters. The total amount of home-
grown wheat will be only about 5,500,000 quarters,
leaving nearly 24,000,000 quarters to be imported."
This works out that last year eighty-three persons
out of every hundred in this country subsisted on
imported wheat.

The following figures, only going back nine years,
invite serious reflection.

Acres planted in wheat in Great Britain :—

1884	...	...	...	...	...	2,667,000
1889	...	...	...	...	...	2,449,000
1890	...	...	...	...	...	2,386,000
1891	...	...	...	...	...	2,300,000
1893	...	...	...	...	...	1,992,000

With an ever-increasing importation of finished manufactured goods, without doubt the exportation of
like articles of British manufacture has most seriously
declined.

Let all who doubt my assertion, that Protected
countries undersell us in the British home market,
study carefully the Board of Trade returns, and they
will find that in hardware, glass, paper, leather, sugar,
silks, woollens, and many other articles of general
use, our markets are invaded by the products of Protectionist countries, and so British labour is robbed to
pay foreign labour.

It is impossible to exaggerate the seriousness of
the position thus indicated. Let Britons pause and
reflect, then take action to arrest the downward
movement.

The hour of national crisis will sooner or later be

upon us, and if we are not speedily aroused to see the danger, *it may be too late to avert the catastrophe.*

The agriculture and manufactures of Great Britain are in a perilous state, and the only remedy to avail is a policy ot National Protection.

CHAPTER XVII.

THE INCIDENCE OF IMPORT TAXATION, OR, WHO PAYS IT?

A very "Simple" Illustration—The Secretary of the Cobden Club asked to explain the Incidence of Import Duties if placed upon certain *Competing* Manufactures — What Bradford Manufacturers find out, in Practice—A Nut for the "Free Trade" Reader to Crack—The Lessons learnt by Practical Business Experience—The Registration Duty on Corn—The Abolition of the Indian Import Duties on Cotton Goods at the Instance of Lancashire Manufacturers —The Cat again let out of the Bag—The United Kingdom exceeds every other Country in Europe in the Extent of her Custom-house Duties—On Non-competing Products ; every Import similar to Anything we can Produce at Home must come in Free—How we Protect Foreign Labour against British Labour in the British Market—Much Considered British Consumer Paying nearly 500 Millions Sterling Duties on Tea, Tobacco, Coffee and Dried Fruits in Fifty Years —Taking off Taxes—Following a Will-o'-the-wisp Policy.

WHO pays the duties levied on imports? The average Free Trader will rejoin, in his rule-of-thumb way, "Why, of course, the country imposing them."

Turning to a Cobden Club publication, "Richard Cobden," by Richard Gowing, I find the following :—

"The Earl of Ripon, at the unveiling of the Cobden statue at Stockport in 1886, demonstrated the fallacy of the theory that the foreign producer pays the import duty, by the simple illustration of the English duty on tea ; if the Chinese producer paid the English duty, then our tea would have been none the cheaper for the large reductions of duty which have brought the market down to one-third of the old prices."

This simple—very simple—illustration is supposed to settle the whole question, once for all (from the Cobdenite point of view), of the incidence of import taxation.

Now, the article tea is not produced in this country, and when the importation is taxed we absolutely increase the cost to the extent of the tax, and all incidental charges it creates.   The reason is simple enough, because there is no competition in production to correct the action of the duty, therefore, the tax on tea is to all intents and purposes a direct tax on individual consumers.   (If our fiscal policy implied imperial commercial federation of the British empire, tea from British possessions would be received under a preferential rate of duty—*i.e.*, assuming that it was deemed advisable to continue a duty on this popular article of general consumption.)

The secretary of the Cobden Club (Mr. Gowing) prudently refrained from going outside a non-competing article for his illustration ; such is the grasp of the subject by an official of the society which exists for the purpose of keeping the lamp of truth burning in our midst.

I now turn to the Free Traders' pet industry— cotton manufactures (for the *supposed* benefit of which Englishmen deliberately sacrificed their greatest in-

dustrial interest—agriculture), and let us presume that
we taxed the importation of cotton goods (about £3
millions per annum), say 20 per cent. *ad valorem ;*
by so doing the consumers of cotton goods in this
country would not pay a fraction of the import duty.
Why? Because our production is about five times
our consumption, and, therefore, all imported must be
invoiced plus the 20 per cent. duty to compete with
prices in the home market. If the importations continued, the foreign producer would pay the duty, or
if unable to continue the trade, then our own work-
people would enjoy to the full extent the value of the
home market.

We imported, in 1893 (see Chapter XIV.), watches
and clocks = £1,161,807 ; gloves and boots =
£2,495,531 ; leather dressed = £6,581,142 ; paper =
£2,347,080 ; glass = £2,443,259 ; iron = £3,007,062 ;
silk manufactures = £12,026,616 ; woollen manufactures = £12,081,754 ; mixed cloth = £607,241.   It
would be interesting to know how Mr. Gowing ex-
plained, *on business principles*, the incidence of import
duties if placed upon this enormous volume of *competing* manufactures.

If Bradford manufacturers find, in practice, that
they have been paying American duties, why should
not Belgian, French, and German manufacturers,
their productions being met with import duties at
United Kingdom ports, experience the same thing?
Under these conditions, one of two things must
happen ; either the continental producers would contribute to our imperial revenue, or they would lose
that control of our markets which is secured to them

by our present one-sided system of free competing imports.

Again, let me take an example of exporting some commodity to America, a commodity we can produce under favourable conditions, something we are eager to send to America.   If there is no duty on the importation, and the price, according to supply and demand, rules at, say, 20s. per cwt., we shall have to put our article quality for quality into an American port, freight and expenses paid at 19s. per cwt.; but the cute Yankee (wishing to develop the production of this particular commodity, furnishing employment to American labour, and adding to national wealth, the whole value of the product being spent in America and forming spendable revenue to her citizens) places 5s. per cwt. on the import.   How will the English manufacturer or merchant (under the altered conditions) invoice his article?   He cannot charge 24s., because the price rules 20s. in America (fixed by production and consumption), and he is bound to invoice at 14s., *i.e.*, plus the import duty, assuming business is done.   Who, in this instance, pays the tax?   Of course the people engaged in production on this side. I respectfully ask the careful attention of my Free Trade reader to this example; let him try and crack the nut.

There is the case of exporting steel rails to America. When we could not invoice them plus the duty, the trade fell down, because the whole business turned upon the volume of production in America.   And this must be so all the world over, hence the supreme importance of each country developing its own pro-

ducing forces. It is all very well for Free Traders to
shout the foreigner sends us this " very cheap " and
that " very cheap "; the foreigner does not send us
anything because he loves us. Oh, no, he puts it in
at just such a price as will take the market. *This is
the lesson we learn by practical business experience,
the test we should apply to every fiscal measure.*

As illustrative of this test I have only to refer to
one or two well-known instances of our own experience. The registration duty on corn, which was
continued up to 1869, did not add one farthing to the
price of wheat to the British consumer. At 1s. per
quarter it yielded to the revenue no less a sum than
one million sterling on the then very moderate volume
of our imports per annum. Its abolition, at the
instance of the demands of speculative importers,
deprived the nation of this revenue and transferred
its burden from the shoulders of the foreign producer
(for the money had still to be raised) to those of the
British tax-payer. As a matter of fact, beyond cavil
or doubt, the market price of wheat was not reduced
the slightest fraction by the abrogation of that duty;
the gain was entirely absorbed by the foreign growers,
and those interested in the foreign trade. The same
was the case with the abolition of the Indian import
duties on cotton goods at the instance of the Lancashire manufacturers.

It is too preposterous to assume that these astute
individuals supposed for a moment that the Indian
consumer paid any portion of these duties ; the
Indian exchequer, to its sorrow and embarrassment,
lost in the event a natural and fertile source of revenue,

and had to fall back upon opium licences, salt taxes, and Economies which forbade the investment of British capital in Indian railways, and the due development of the means of communication. And now, when, as a result of the financial and political difficulties resulting from that blunder, these duties have to be re-imposed, the cat is again let out of the bag by Lancashire again selfishly demanding " protection " by being exempted from the operation of the duties. *But why claim this exemption if the consumer paid the tax?*

English people have talked about free breakfast tables, free education, etc., but the fact remains, that the United Kingdom exceeds every other country in Europe in the extent of her custom-house duties. We raise some £20 millions annually on *non*-competing products; every import similar to anything we can produce at home must come in free, and whatever we cannot produce may be taxed exorbitantly; in this way we protect foreign labour against British labour in the British market.

Foreign countries do the reverse of our plan, for they adjust their revenue duties to *benefit internal trade* and *industry*.

It is, indeed, difficult to understand why our insane system should be continued for a single year longer. The experience of Protectionist countries has completely established the fact that, on such articles as a country can itself produce, a duty, from the keen internal competition engendered, does not act injuriously to the consumer.

Much considered British consumer! let us see how

N

he has fared. From the Statistical Abstracts I
gather that he has had to pay, during the fifty years
ending 1890,

On Tea ...	...	...	...	...	£181,874,135
On Tobacco	...	...	...	...	290,575,145
On Coffee	...	...	...	...	13,951,874
On Dried Fruits		...	...	...	7,749,246
					£494,150,400

A nice little lump of money towards John Bull's
standing expenses—and to give the foreigner the
benefit of a free market!

What a fuss was made about the import duty on
corn, which, *during the whole thirty-four years of its
existence, only amounted to £9,900,000, or £292,000
per annum*, which was, as a question of fact, not paid
by the British consumer, but by the foreigner.

During our palmy trading days, Mr. Gladstone
indulged in "taking off taxes." The press and the
public shouted in exultation, extolling the "great
master of finance." It was only a red-herring business, but it had the desired effect, *i.e.*, catching votes.
However taking on the surface, it was merely a
shuffling of the cards, heaping up direct, and freeing
indirect, taxation. Mr. Gladstone's clever finance
developed free imports, and thereby ruined many
British trades. *He strengthened foreign labour, robbed
British labour, and generally weakened the resources of
the State.*

Taxation—imperial and local—has mounted up to
such proportions during recent years that the fairness

and public policy of our present system of raising money is sure to become, at an early date, a topic of general controversy. Direct taxation has had its day of fashion, but it looks as if the tax-payers of Great Britain have had enough of it. Such is the poverty of our resources that, whenever a few extra millions are wanted (to protect our food supplies from foreign countries), the payers of income tax have to bear the brunt of it. In fact, John Bull is finding his standing expenses a very heavy burden ; his position is painful ; he has melancholy experiences, and, just now, feels dispirited with gloomy anticipations ; he is wearied and disgusted with political battledore and shuttlecock. Instead of *union*, he observes disintegration and decomposition, and a general disorganisation of his national industries, a slough of misery, into which he has drifted by following a Will-o'-the-wisp policy—a policy which consists of combining things which are essentially irreconcilable.

CHAPTER XVIII.

EMIGRATION. THE VALUE OF BRITISH COLONIES.

The Exportation of the Flower of the Working Classes—A Bit
of Satire — Statistics of Emigration, 1849-1892—Britain
stands solitary among the Nations—John Bull's many Resources for the Full and Varied Employment of his People
—John Bull's Colossal Possessions Abroad— How to insure
" Unity " to the British Empire, and raise up New Markets
and New Customers—The Teaching of the Manchester
School of Politicians made " British Citizenship" an Idle
Word—A Declaration of Professor Goldwin Smith—" Little
England " Politicians —A Fool's Paradise of Visionary Expectations—The English Government "has no Business
with Emigration;" like Everything Else, it must be "left to
settle Itself"—Cosmopolitanism taking the Place of Patriot-
ism—Emigration a Necessity under our Suicidal Fiscal
System — A Working Man's Question—Lord Salisbury and
an Imperial Policy—Is the Heart of the Nation Sound ?—
Loyalty and Patriotism—The *Conservation* of the Empire
—The *Scum* upon the Surface—A Great Opportunity.

EMIGRATION is one of the great social problems of
the day. The stream of emigration has gone on with
steady persistence for many years. The stream of
labour, the best bone and sinew of the British Isles,
the shrewd workers and skilled artisans, have left our
shores to establish industries abroad—mainly in the
States of the American Union.

They have turned their backs upon the "blessings"
of Free Trade, and gone to a country where their
labour is protected. The paupers, and loafers, and
ne'er-do-weels remain at home. Under the Free

Trade patent for impoverishing and pauperising the nation, a glorious discovery has been made, that a country must be depopulated to be enriched. Drive out the workers—the able-bodied who produce ; the old, the puny, the infirm, the idlers can remain. The exportation of the flower of the working classes, coupled with the importation of destitute aliens, are the outward and visible signs of " prosperity " under our " blessed " Free Trade system ! This bit of satire is warranted by an utterance, a few years ago, of that eminent Free Trade statistician, Mr. Giffen : " The general increase in emigration to the United States may no doubt be considered as an additional sign of the revival of trade." That is, as soon as our workers can get their passage money in their pockets, they desert our shores.

We may well ask, If this is a sign of prosperity for Free Trade England, what must be the yet more exceeding prosperity of the United States, that has induced so many emigrants to leave the old country and the old flag ? [1] Millions of British subjects have

[1] Number of Emigrants, of British and Irish Origin, from the United Kingdom to Countries out of Europe.

	Emigrants to U.S.A.	Total Emigration.
1849-54	1,378,096	1,938,443
1855-69	1,788,068	2,639,739
1870-84	1,945,698	2,966,095
1885-92	1,316,527	1,902,419
	* 6,428,389	9,446,696

* Not including those who have made their way through Canada.

Population of the United Kingdom, 1849 ...	27,669,579
„ „ „ „ 1892 ...	38,014,973
Increase in 43 years ...	10,345,394

given up their allegiance, and become citizens under the stars and stripes. The United States have been strengthened, and the British Empire weakened by the exodus.

In this peculiar madness of emigration, Britain stands solitary among the nations. She gets rid of her defenders in sending away her peasantry and artisans, and offers a premium for national decay and dry-rot.

John Bull has many resources for the employment of his people. "John Bull's Blessings" are referred to by a writer in *Chambers's Journal*, May, 1865, who was intent upon showing that "the British Islands are more favourably circumstanced in relation to the phenomena on which material welfare depends than any other part of the earth." He wrote:—"We have an unusual amount of sea-coast in proportion to the superficial area of the kingdom. This at once gives a most important increase of facilities for fishing, for shipbuilding, for establishing docks and harbours, for exporting our surplus produce and manufactures, for importing those of other countries." Speaking of the equability of our climate:—"Man here *must* work, because the temperature is free alike from excessive degrees of heat and cold."

And writing of the geology of the British Isles:— "The geological formation is far above the average richness in mineral treasures. Iron is the backbone of nineteenth century civilisation, and fuel is the pabulum on which the giant feeds; and steam is the fluid which circulates through his veins. Who can measure the full effects of our coal deposits on Eng-

land's greatness? . . . . The supply is enough for
smelting all our enormous quantities of iron, for
smelting our copper and tin, for casting and forging
all the numberless productions in metal, for supplying
all our factory steam-engines, for keeping alight the
fires of all our locomotives and steamships, for giving
a cheerful blaze to millions of fire-places; and after
doing all this, we have enough to spare for a large
supply to foreign countries. . . . . It gives bread to a
vast number of people, who transfer it to every part
of the kingdom. Then the quarries of stone for
engineering and building purposes; the slate for
vessels and for roofs; the fire-clay for furnaces and
retorts; the pottery clay suitable for the finest porce-
lain; the beds of salt for which nearly every European
nation envies us, and which we really do not fully
appreciate because we never experience the want of
it; the alum which Yorkshire and Scotland supply;
the exhaustless abundance of clay suitable for making
bricks; the equally exhaustless stores of limestone
and chalk, so invaluable for making concrete, cement,
and mortar; the sand and the alkali necessary for
making all the varieties of glass; of all these gifts
the British Islands contain within their bosom such a
bounteous store that millions of men find profitable
employment in bringing them into useful form."

John Bull possesses, in fact, all the material elements of wealth—a splendid combination of circumstances arising out of natural and physical causes.
Surely he should be strong upon his legs with a good
constitution. Passing away from John Bull's resources at home, let us take a brief glance at his

colossal possessions abroad. There is the magnificent Indian Empire, with products of inexhaustible profusion, boundless natural riches, giving the means of purchase for British goods.

Cast our eyes to the West and we see the Dominion of Canada (with a territory about equal to that of the United States) containing limitless forests of fine timber, fertile agricultural areas, provinces capable of wheat production to any extent, and possessing the finest harbours in the world. Cape Breton, Prince Edward's Island, and the Hudson Bay territory, the West Indian Islands—suggestive of abundant sugar supplies—Jamaica, Barbadoes, Trinidad, Demarara, the Bahamas, the Bermuda Islands, South Africa and the West Coast of Africa, etc. Again, look away at the vast continent of Australia, New Zealand, etc. This is an incomplete and imperfect sketch of the dominions of the British Crown— Greater Britain—an empire possessing all the elements of strength and durability. *The one thing needful is statesmanship to consolidate this empire into a vast Imperial confederation, based upon fiscal preferences.* We have within our reach unlimited production, purchase and trade ; we have a great family, but a *truly Imperial policy* is needed to unite the members of this great family.

I leave to the concluding chapter an exposition of principles calculated to ensure *unity* to the British Empire ; unity that implies aid and sympathy in times of difficulty and trial to all British subjects throughout the world.

In that chapter I shall explain how British

markets can be made available to Britishers, how our colonial trade can employ surplus capital to the greatest advantage, and raise up new markets and new customers.

Unfortunately, we have had our anti-colonial, cosmopolitan, and disintegrating theories. Instead of binding the empire into *one Great British Zolverein*, we have preferred to trade with foreign countries with their hostile tariffs, and made ourselves ridiculous in the eyes of the world with foreign treaty engagements.

[1] Our cosmopolitan Free Trade system has been unsuited to our colonies, and must, so long as we stand by it, tend to the loosening instead of the drawing closer the bond of union between them and us.

The teaching of the Manchester School of politicians made " British citizenship " an idle word.

Mr. Cobden, in 1842, referring to the colonial system, " with all its dazzling appeals to the passions of the people," urged Free Trade " to gradually and imperceptibly loosen the bands which unite our colonies to us by a mistaken notion of self-interest." Again, to show how, some twenty-five years ago, England had lost the right estimation of her special art, and vital interest in colonisation, *i.e., community and partnership*, I bring to light a declaration of Professor Goldwin Smith :

" That our possessions, if regarded as military posts, must be abandoned, because in these days of Free Trade commerce no longer needs cannon to clear her path ; but if regarded as colonies they must be

[1] See Chapter XIX., "Commercial Treaties with Foreign States."

abandoned, because in adopting Free Trade we have destroyed the only motive for retaining our colonies."

It was the deliberate policy of Cobden to bring about a separation, and even the chiefs at the colonial office encouraged by significant suggestions some colonies to ask for independence; in fact, the policy was to incite and *goad* colonies to that end, by an irregular and inconsistent course of action. There were irritations, recriminations, heartburnings, and antagonistic feelings towards our great self-governing colonies.

This school of politicians spoke of the costliness of maintaining colonies, and being rid of responsibility for them. We had administrators who regarded the colonies as rather elements of weakness to us than of strength. There was no endeavour to develop their resources, or send them the overflow of our population. The policy of twenty-five years ago was to educate the colonies in self-dependence, so that they could start on their own account. In a word, shake off the colonies. In the minds of these " Little England " politicians the mother country was to cast off communities of her children, no matter if England sank dishonoured in the estimation of the whole world, having forfeited the prestige acquired by so lavish an expenditure of blood and treasure in times past.

These Free Trade politicians lived in a fool's paradise of visionary expectations. To divert trade, or the overflow of our population, to British colonies was doing violence to the sacred principles of Free Trade political economy. Everything must find its level naturally ; so said the apostles of *laissez-faire*. In this way English Governments have been profoundly indifferent how the people have been cast adrift. Their attitude is unexampled in the history of mankind.

If France or Germany possessed colonies like Great Britain, their Governments would have made the utmost use of them for purposes of trade and emigration.

The English Government "*has no business with emigration.*" It, like everything else, must be "left to settle itself."

What folly ! We have every resource in our colonies. We have land, capital, and labour, yet no effort must be made to bring them together.

Cosmopolitanism has taken the place of patriotism. Shame upon the pettifogging politicians who have disregarded our precious inheritance, and sent millions of our people to foreign States instead of attaching them to the empire !

Shame upon political charlatans who have scattered abroad the fragments of a great nation, and cast away the roots and branches of the old British oak !

Let Englishmen rise up and dismiss these treasonable apostles of *laissez-faire*, and, in future, act upon principles of *utility* as regards our inter-imperial trade and emigration.

Protect the labour of Great Britain and Ireland, and then, if there is a surplus of population, spread that surplus over British colonies. Englishmen and Irishmen in Australia, or Canada, or the Cape, will not

forfeit their nationality ; and more, they will have love
in their hearts towards the mother country ; they will
multiply, and give essential strength to the British
Empire.

Let Englishmen declare at the polls that their
magnificent empire shall be *built up*, and *not broken to
pieces*.

Emigration is a necessity under our suicidal fiscal
policy.   The present condition of our industries cannot possibly maintain the population—our people
must be drafted off somewhere.   Are they to go to
British colonies, or attach themselves to a foreign
State ?

This is a question for all ranks of society—especially for the working men.   We cry out for new markets, when the markets of the empire are capable of
unlimited expansion.   We have annexed Burmah, we
are opening up Africa, we hold Egypt, but as much
for foreign States as ourselves.

I charge doctrinaire politicians with the fatal
error of sending millions of Irishmen to the United
States of America, to breed discontent and rebellion.
It is the duty of every right-minded citizen to see
that our future policy is such, that the working
people of this country are *not* broken down with disappointment and neglect, that they are not further
compelled to follow the Irish example.

Lord Salisbury cannot be ignorant of the vast
issues involved in the question of an Imperial policy
for the empire, for he said, at Birmingham, in March,
1883 :—

"Again, do not listen to the ridiculous pretence that

those who are jealous for the great empire of England abroad are actuated by the miserable and narrow considerations belonging to a particular class. In our belief, the great empire which we have inherited from the exertions of our forefathers concerns all alike ; but it concerns those most who depend most for the constancy of trade and employment upon the constant prosperity of the country. We do not believe that an England stripped of India, stripped of its colonies, humbled before Europe, would be a happy England for the working classes. We have received from the self-denial and heroic actions of our forefathers a great empire. We mean, if we can, to keep it, to develop it, to strengthen it, to enrich it, and that not in the interest of one class, but of all, and most of all of the industrial classes of this country."

Loyalty and patriotism have worked wonders for us in times past, and might again. Will it be so ? Is the heart of the nation sound ? Can we consider that the fallacious political theories treated upon in this chapter are existent only from an accidental state of things, and will have no abiding place in the history of our country ? If the bulk of our fellow countrymen have not seriously considered the situation, it is high time that they had ; if we are an order-loving people, desiring permanence and stability to our nation and empire, we must use the present time wisely, and close our ranks against disunion and that political wrangling which is making English politics the laughing-stock of the civilised world. The working classes now have political power in their hands, let us hope that it will be used for their good—and the good of the commonwealth.

Protection *versus* Free Trade must be fought out in the political arena ; Protection is what every English workman calls for in one form or another. Animated with loyalty and patriotism, the workers will demand a Government which will secure the wide range of the empire for the Britons' benefit, and dismiss the Government detected in spending the nation's time over peddling party affairs. This will come to pass if Englishmen are not permanently be-witched. The cry for Protection implies *conservation* of the empire, for Imperial commercial federation of the empire is the sequel to the protection of native labour against the products of foreign labour when offered for sale in the home market.

However, the Radical and Socialistic following do not seem intent on the conservation of the empire ; they are doing their best to ruin the land of England, and to ruin the manufactures of England ; and as to the British Empire, well, a noted labour leader is reported as saying, " The empire could go to a hotter place than a baker's shop for all he cared." Let us hope that this is only the *scum* upon the surface of our national life. The electors of England would be fools indeed to exchange the British Empire for ANARCHY.

Anarchy ought not to have any place in the hearts of Englishmen. It, and Radical Socialism, however dissimilar, can only be met with *an Imperial policy ;* there is no other policy that has a promise of great-ness and security. " Union is strength." But if

Englishmen go on cutting each others' throats, and rifling each others' property, national effacement will be in store for them.

If loyalty and patriotism are non-existent in the hearts of Englishmen, they are lost for ever. May the consideration of the subject of this chapter temper and guide our line of action in the great crisis which is at hand.

A great opportunity presents itself for consolidating on a permanent basis the *union of the empire*, an opportunity which, if allowed to pass away, might never return, for a bond of common allegiance—the strength of *union* in a great empire.

CHAPTER XIX.

COMMERCIAL TREATIES WITH FOREIGN STATES.

Two Things stand in the Way—The Reflected Prosperity
Doctrine—The French Postal Convention of 1856—The
Special Privileges accorded to Foreign Vessels in British
Colonial Ports—How does the Foreigner treat Vessels
under the British Flag?—The Manchester Chamber of
Commerce Resolution of July 30, 1888—Lord Knutsford's
Reply—Cobden's Treaty and the Ruin of the British Silk
Industry—The "Unlucky" Treaties of 1862 and 1865, and
our Position under them—Lord Salisbury's Reply to a Depu-
tation—Another Resolution passed by the Manchester Cham-
ber of Commerce—The Great Vice of our Treaty-Mongering
—Giving Bread, but pelted with Stones—How "Favoured
Treatment" is obtained—Foreign Countries give their
Colonies Preferential Treatment—In the Name of Common
Sense why should we not have the Liberty to do likewise?
Guarding against Future Entanglements—Copies of Letters
from Sir S. W. Griffiths and Sir S. L. Tilley—The Recent
Inter-Colonial Conference at Ottawa—The Moral—Mr.
Rhodes is not to be put down.

THERE are two things which stand in the way of
Imperial commercial federation of the British Empire
—1. The system of (so-called) Free Trade. 2. Our
commercial treaty obligations with foreign countries.

When we are prepared to do violence to that
political curiosity (Free Trade), then will be untied
the bonds which have enslaved our possessions beyond the seas.

When we have ceased to be ethereal dreamers of

cosmopolitan paradises, the first thing Englishmen will do will be to get free from the entanglements of existing treaties, and assert their just rights of treating the empire as a whole.

The mad policy of the Manchester School implied making foreign countries prosperous so that we could enjoy their reflected prosperity. This reflected prosperity doctrine should be viewed in the light, that if it is good enough for us, let it be good enough for foreign States. The story of 1846 is an illustration of the "dog and shadow." Certainly our prosperity will not come by treating British colonies as outside the pale of imperial and commercial consideration. This was the case under the old world treaties of the Cobden School, although, to be logical, Free Trade should have nothing to do with treaties at all. But further, how can you bargain when you have not anything to bargain with?[1]

The first of our absurd commercial treaty engage-

[1] Great Britain has nothing to bargain with under Free Trade policy. That is, nothing legitimate to bargain with. As the sequel of these pages shows, the treaty-mongering Free Trade politicians (they were not statesmen any more than patriots) bargained with the rights and the property of British citizenship, treasonably conferring privileges upon foreign States at the expense of our colonies, and of our vast industrial interests at home.

For want of the legitimate bargaining power which a wise fiscal and Imperial policy would have conferred, they gave away in bribes the heritage of the British people. This is the sorry bargaining power of one-sided Free Trade to dispossess the British producer of the value of the inheritance acquired at such cost of blood and treasure, and confer it, for illusory advantages, upon our Protectionist competitors abroad.

ments with foreign States was the French Postal
Convention of September, 1856, which accorded
special privileges to foreign mail steamers in British
colonial ports over British steamers. The special
privileges (appertaining to vessels of war) included
the freedom from search, from arrest, from the juris-
diction of the Colonial Admiralty Courts, or any
judge in the colonies, and the freedom from the application of the Habeas Corpus Act with respect to the
ship's passengers.

German vessels claimed the same privileges to the
distinct disadvantage and loss of prestige of vessels
flying the British flag.

It is curious how we could, in 1856, have given
such privileges, but the circumstances of that period
afford an explanation. France had been our close
ally in the Crimea, and we were on excellent terms
with her emperor. Very soon came the Convention.
John Bull had a notion that these things would become reciprocal. In those days he (J. B.) was very
prosperous, and grew magnanimous ; he was surfeited
with his prosperity and affected benevolence and
cosmopolitanism. John treated the foreigner with
great liberality in British colonial ports, but the
foreigner has not reciprocated. How does the
foreigner treat vessels under the British flag ? In
Italian ports goods in Italian bottoms are admitted
on more favourable terms than those of other nations.
Spain extends this practice to all her colonies, the
only exception being coal cargoes. The United
States close their trade between the Atlantic sea-
board and the Pacific seaboard entirely and absolutely

against all nations, on the ground that it is " coasting," and for United States ships only. France desires to import all produce direct from the countries of production through her own ports. Her policy has regard to the circumstances of origin ; hence cotton, wool, silk, sugar, rice, etc., if shipped from United Kingdom ports are met with the surtax of entrepôt, and by so doing this has impaired England's famous entrepôt trade of former years. British shipowners have to face exacting and vexatious French brokerage laws. The writer brought this subject before the attention of the Manchester Chamber of Commerce on July 30th, 1888, and carried *(nem. con.)* a resolution that :—" This Chamber is of opinion that the conditions of competition are unjust and prejudicial to British interests." On a copy of the resolution being sent to the Secretary of State to the colonies, the following reply was forwarded to the Secretary of the Manchester Chamber of Commerce :—

" *Copy.*
" DOWNING STREET,
" 11*th May*, 1889.

" SIR,—With reference to your letter of the 30th of July last, relating to the special privileges accorded to foreign mail steamers in British colonial ports, I am directed by Lord Knutsford to acquaint you, for the information of the Manchester Chamber of Commerce, that those privileges will be withdrawn, after the 30th of April next, 1890, owing to the termination on that date of the French Convention of September, 1856.—I am, Sir, your obedient servant,
" (Signed) EDWARD WINGFIELD."

So much for the Postal Convention of 1856. Cobden's French Treaty was passed in January, 1860, when the British silk industry was suddenly exposed to unrestricted foreign competition.

Let Coventry, Macclesfield, Congleton, Derby, Leek, etc., speak as to the miseries inflicted by Cobden's Treaty. Judged by results, it was a cruel, insane act, and cannot possibly be defended.

I pass on to examine further treaty-mongering, namely, the two unlucky treaties enslaving us by favoured nation treatment—1862 and 1865.

" 1862.—Treaty of Commerce with Belgium, article 15, expressly states : ' Articles, the produce or manufacture of Belgium, shall not be subject in the British Colonies to other or higher duties than those which are, or may be, imposed upon similar articles of British origin.' "

" 1865.—Treaty of commerce with the Zollverein, article 11, the goods of either of which ' in particular shall be subject to no higher or other duties than the produce and manufactures of any third country the most favoured in those respects.'   Article 7, that ' the stipulations of the preceding articles, 1 to 6, also be applied to the Colonies and foreign possessions of her Britannic Majesty.' "

Thus, the position of Great Britain and her colonies, under the Belgian and German treaties, is " that goods from those countries with whom we are under treaty engagements shall not be subject to higher duties in British colonies than are levied upon similar articles from the United Kingdom, and *vice-versa*." This, undoubtedly, is a fair and exact interpretation of the treaties named; and, under these circumstances, preferential treatment of British colonies is impossible. Under most favoured nation treatment, any concessions made to or by the colonies must be extended to Belgium and Germany, and other countries under treaty engagements.

It is difficult to understand the apathy of Englishmen with regard to treaties made with powers not nearly so important as our great self governing colonies. The sooner we put our house in order the better, and make fiscal union of the empire possible. Why should Englishmen be deprived of their just rights of treating the empire as a whole?

If Great Britain has left her colonies unconsidered, foreign countries have not done so with theirs.

British statesmen in their estimate of the strength, present and future, of Great Britain should consider the value of commercial union with Britain's magnificent possessions. The adoption of this Imperial policy would imply that all *production* within the limits of the British Empire should stimulate re-production within the same area, and be an absolute addition to the wealth of that empire.

Statesmen animated with this grand idea of imperial commercial federation would exhibit a striking contrast to the present-day halting and craven politicians, living in fear of Socialism or a graduated income tax.

We are scouring the world for fresh markets for our exports when we possess (we have control of over 11,000,000) over 8,000,000 square miles of imperial

territory, with over 300,000,000 of British subjects.
We have vast colonies, peopled by our own kindred,
anxious to trade with us, but with no commercial
understanding or tie.   Is it rational, is it sensible, to
give our colonies no advantages over foreign countries
in our commercial relations with them ?   The British
Empire is vast enough, and productive enough, for all
its requirements, but, until the United Kingdom
ceases to treat its colonies as foreign States, and shows
some willingness to enter into reciprocal fiscal arrangements with them, it will never reap the benefit of its
own strength.   The initiative must come from the
mother country, and not from the colonies.   This is
the natural and reasonable course.

It is quite clear that a patriotic policy will not
permit commercial treaties and conventions with
foreign countries which clash with trade arrangements
with our colonies.

Our great men at the head of political parties may
talk of the difficulties in the way, but the time will
certainly come when the development of the resources
of the British Empire will be deemed of more importance—politically and commercially—than restricted,
hap-hazard intercourse with foreign States.

The German States became a great Germanic confederation by means of fiscal arrangements.   The
States of the American Union were brought together
in like fashion.   The scattered Settlements of Canada
became a dominion owing to a measure of Protection,
carried through by the decisive action of a single
mind (Canada's Grand Old Man).   Now, with the
accomplishment of these federations, why should not

the whole British Empire be federated—commercially, industrially, and politically? Notice should be given for the termination of the treaties of 1862 and 1865.

Lord Salisbury, receiving a deputation in June, 1891, respecting these treaties, remarked :—

" I am sure the matter of our relations with our colonies could not have been fully considered. We have tried to find out from official records what the species of reasoning was that induced the statesmen of that day to sign such very unfortunate pledges, but I don't think they had any notion that they were signing any pledges at all."

The interests of the empire demand that the ban of the treaties should be removed ; and it is a pity that Lord Salisbury does not stand forward as a leader, with the decisive action of his great mind, and turn popular opinion into the right direction, but he is under the tyranny of Free Trade superstition, and has before his eyes the fear of offending his Free Trade allies. Having in mind the obnoxious provisions of the treaties in question, the writer decided to bring the subject before the notice of the Manchester Chamber of Commerce, by resolution ; and, accordingly, at the quarterly meeting, held April 28, 1890, moved :—

" That in the opinion of this Chamber no treaties of commerce should in future be concluded unless a clause be therein inserted, to the effect that the deferential treatment of its colonies by any power shall *not* be considered action of a nature to justify any claim by the other contracting party or parties, under the most favoured nation clause."

The writer then stated that the great vice of the
treaty system in the past was that political considerations had entered too much into the negotiations, that
our politicians, in their diplomatic inducements, had
passed over our great industrial and trading interests.
They, one and all, appeared to have had a burning
desire to distinguish their term of office by affixing
their signature to some treaty, whatever be its
character.   That commercial interests had suffered
owing to political exigencies, concessions having been
granted on our side from time to time, which foreign
States had readily seized upon, to our great disadvantage.

In fact, foreign States were continually placing
restrictions upon British trade—" We had given them
bread, and, in return for our cosmopolitan policy, had
been pelted with stones."

The much vaunted most favoured nation clause was
examined, and it was shown that this favoured treatment is not secured under our present fiscal arrangements, but obtained in the first place by some country
in virtue of a policy the antipodes of our own, which
has forced another State to give it.   Thus, although
our Government failed in 1881 to renew the Anglo-
French Treaty, it has since received from France the
most favoured nation treatment.   Which simply
means that France gives us no advantage over the
conventional tariff which she has already yielded to
other contracting countries.   The most favoured nation
treatment sounds well; it tickles the ear, but its advantages to Great Britain are more apparent than
real.

We have already seen that this favoured nation clause precludes us from giving preferential treatment to our colonies and possessions abroad, as it is quite evident that foreign countries are under the impression that it is not merely the United Kingdom they are dealing with, but, practically, the British Empire, with all its dependencies and possessions. As regards our self-governing colonies, it is doubtful if the home Government can really bind them by any foreign treaty, for having control of their own fiscal policy they might repudiate such treaty. This has not been done so far, but, under certain circumstances, action of this sort may be taken.

We know that foreign countries, notably France and Spain, give their colonies preferential treatment in their home markets. They do not, in any way, consider our susceptibilities. *In the name of common sense, why should we not have the liberty to do likewise ?*

In executing a treaty, why should other countries have advantages not shared in by ourselves ? Now, what would foreign countries (with whom we are under treaty engagements) say if our self-government colonies (Protectionist in policy) yielded special concessions to the mother country ? Certainly they would take action of some sort. The resolution at the Manchester Chamber of Commerce was intended to dispel all doubts as to the interpretation of the 1862 and 1865 treaties, and the *proviso* contained in the resolution (if carried into effect) guarded against entanglement should any further treaty be entered upon ; it also paved the way for adopting such a commercial policy towards our colonies as would tend to the maintaining and strengthening of the whole British Empire.

The Chamber passed the resolution, and ordered copies of it to be sent to the Prime Minister, as Secretary of State for Foreign Affairs, and also to the Secretary of State for the Colonies. The writer received many letters of congratulation on the resolution being carried. Among them were the following :—

MERTHYR, BRISBANE,
QUEENSLAND, *June* 18, 1890.

DEAR SIR,—I am much obliged for the reprint of the proceedings of the Manchester Chamber of Commerce, containing the resolution unanimously adopted on the subject of commercial treaties with foreign Powers, and for the other reprints that you were good enough to send me, which I have read with great interest.

The resolution *is most satisfactory*, especially as being passed *in Manchester;* but I *should like to see* it passed in the *House of Commons*.

I confess that I have a difficulty in understanding the apathy with which this subject is regarded by statesmen in England. They cannot, or they will not, understand the real conditions of the Empire they have to govern, or if they do they are *affrighted at the fetish of " Free-trade."*

I sincerely hope that they will awake to the actual necessities of the situation before it is too late—a time which may come sooner than is expected if nothing is done.—Yours very faithfully,   (Signed)   S. W. GRIFFITHS.

To Edwin Burgis, Esq., Manchester.

GOVERNMENT HOUSE,
ST. JOHN, N.B., *June* 7, 1890.

DEAR SIR,—I have to thank you for the reprint of recent proceedings at the Manchester Chamber of Commerce, and as a friend of *confederation of the Empire* I thank you for having

secured the passage of the resolution bearing upon the question of commercial treaties with foreign countries.—Yours faithfully,
(Signed)   S. L. TILLEY.
To Edwin Burgis, Esq., Manchester.

The Inter-Colonial Conference—of representatives from the self-governing colonies in Australia, South Africa, and North America—recently held at Ottawa, marks an epoch in the history of the British Empire. It manifests a spirit of Imperialism on the part of these great self-governing colonies, and voices the ideas which have of recent years been gaining ground in the minds of Britons generally.

It is a fine exhibition of unmistakable loyalty and determination to preserve the indissoluble bonds of Imperial solidarity.

Colonial statesmen desire the realisation of an economic programme which is nothing short of an Imperial Zollverein.

All honour to their loyal and patriotic instincts.

The whole time of the conference was devoted to the consideration of questions affecting the economic development of the British Empire—how to utilise the resources of the empire to the greatest advantage. The proceedings were thoroughly business-like, as is shown by the press version of what passed, namely:—

The delegates were unanimous on the four following points :—

1. It is proposed that a survey should be made in order to arrive at an estimate of the cost of laying a Trans-Pacific cable, to be wholly under British control, the colonies and the mother country sharing in the expense of the survey.

2. The Imperial Government is to be "respectfully" asked to contribute to the support of a swift mail service across the North Atlantic from Great Britain to a Canadian port.

3. The Imperial Government is to be asked to agree to the abrogation of such treaties, and clauses in colonial constitutions, as forbid the colonies to make commercial arrangements with one another without regard to foreign Powers.

4. The delegates, speaking for the colonies, express a wish for *such a departure from the Imperial commercial policy of the last two generations as will allow us all to give one another a preference in commerce over States not belonging to the Empire.*

There was some disagreement on the following resolution, which was adopted on the trade question :—

This conference records its belief in the advisability of a Customs arrangement between Great Britain and her colonies by which trade within the Empire may be placed on a more favourable footing than that carried on with foreign countries.

In voting, the conference balloted by colonies, and the resolution was adopted by five votes against three, the Yeas being Canada, Tasmania, Cape Colony, South Australia, and Victoria, and the Nays New South Wales, New Zealand, and Queensland. Another resolution was adopted to the following effect:—

That until the mother country can see her way to enter into a Customs arrangement with her colonies, it is desirable that, when empowered to do so, the colonies of Great Britain, or such of them as are disposed to accede to this view, should take steps *to place each other's produce on a more favoured Customs basis than is accorded to the like products of foreign countries.*

On the suggestion of Mr. Hofmeyr, the South African Customs Union, which includes the independent Transvaal and Orange Free River State, was considered part of the territory.

Not only are the colonies anxious that certain steps should be taken to perfect the means of communication between various parts of the British Empire, but *they press forward for the reversal of Britain's fiscal policy.*

It is impossible to doubt the significance of the vote in favour of an Imperial Customs Union, or Imperial Commercial Federation of the British Empire. The resolutions passed by the conference indicate an important advance on the part of the colonies, and the home Government *must* take it into account, that is, if Her Majesty's advisers are not entirely blind to Imperial considerations.

Briefly, the demand is, that the restrictions imposed by existing commercial treaties shall be removed.

Under the teaching of Bright and Cobden England despised her colonies; *the delegates at Ottawa despise Free Trade, and wish to be relieved of its galling fetters.*

The colonies desire to differentiate in favour of each other's produce and that of the mother country, but the treaties referred to in this chapter forbid it. What reply will the mother country make to the demand for the abrogation of the treaties, to be followed by reciprocity between Great Britain and her colonies, and the adoption of a higher tariff on foreign products? Here is something to engage the attention of the British Electorate, and also the attention of a British Ministry. The Inter-Colonial Conference was the work of the colonies. They inaugurated the movement. Will the people of the United Kingdom join hands and give expression to the idea of economic self-sufficiency? Let them see to it that they do not pass over this grand opportunity; to persevere in a disintegrating policy after the plainest warnings would be national folly. The attitude of the home Government over Mr. Rhodes' recent proposal is deplorable, and well merits the severe comments of the Cape Prime Minister, contained in his speech in the House of Assembly, Cape Town, June 18th, this year.

Treating upon the correspondence with the Colonial Office with regard to the admission of Cape products free, and a preferential rate for British manufactures over foreign, in the Chartered Company's territories, Mr. Rhodes observed :—

" They (the Government) rejected his suggestion in order to maintain their Free Trade principles! . . . Her Majesty's Government refused to embody his proposals, as to do so would have been opposed to the general fiscal policy, and they could not propose to Parliament special preferential rights of free import for Cape Colony into the Charterland. . . . Holding, as he did, that the future government of the world was a question of tariffs, he thought it a good opportunity to make it a condition that the duties on British manufactures should not be higher than the duties at present imposed in the South African Customs Union. . . . . Hon. gentlemen might say, 'Very well, you have told us what has happened. What is the use of it?' . . . To that he might reply that the matter was not over yet. The views of governments changed, and he had determined to use all his influence to insist upon his views being carried into effect. He could not agree to the rejection of the clause he had proposed. If the House agreed that some return was due to the English people for all their support and help and the protection that their navy furnished, he was of opinion that the best return a colony could make would be to allow their manufactured goods to pass in at a fair rate. . . . . They had been talking in England about three acres and a cow, about liquor legislation, and about the question of local government for Ireland. They spent their whole time on these matters, but *the big question* of the trade of the people they neglected. . . . . See, for instance, the action of the United States, and of France, and of Russia; and yet the most extraordinary thing is that when the English people are offered the privilege that south of the Zambesi their goods shall be admitted for ever on a fair basis, their rulers absolutely refuse it. . . . We know full well that the States south of the Zambesi will join in one system, and the charter possessing a clause that British goods shall never have a tariff higher than our present one, means that South Africa, when one, will grant this right for ever to British goods—and yet they have refused it. I am glad of the opportunity to state this to the House. It will, I hope, be brought home to the English people, for with them rests the final decision. The proposal has, for the time being, been rejected; but, Mr. Speaker, I do not mind that. I mean to fight the clause until the Imperial Government gives in, and I am quite certain that the wiser counsels will ultimately prevail."

No apology is needed for these quotations. The

words of Mr. Rhodes should be read in every British household. Let Britons rise to the magnitude of the subject, and the weak, vacillating politicians who have misruled England's colonial policy will be sent to the right about.

If Mr. Rhodes could come to England and commence a campaign against our abominable commercial treaties with foreign States, England's sons will see justice done to her colonies.

Mr. Rhodes has proved himself to be no coward in dealing with the theorists in high places—who are so sadly lacking in wisdom and foresight. Let him instruct the industrial classes of Great Britain, whose position is so full of difficulty and anxiety, owing to a policy lacking in statesmanship, and incapable of directing national trade in its proper channels. The industrial classes, in the struggle to get a living, are mainly occupied in making their precarious earnings go as far as possible in procuring cheap commodities —they are dispirited, and are in danger of losing their national pride in country and empire.

Statesmen like Mr. Rhodes are princely prophets in directing the democracy of England to the vast heritage purchased by the heroism of England's worthies, in reminding them of unlimited production, purchase, and trade possessed under the dominion of the British flag. The working classes of this country should not remain ignorant of these advantages. After incurring the cost of acquisition of a great Empire, what folly to refuse to reap the benefit! British markets are open to the foreigner without distinction, why not give a preference to British subjects?

CHAPTER XX.

MAINTAIN THE BRITISH EMPIRE BY IMPERIAL COMMERCIAL UNION.

Organic Unity of the British Empire desired—The Necessary
" Solvent Union," its Consideration too long delayed—The
Basis of the " Solvent Union "—Five Subjects claiming
Attention—The First Alternative—Sir John Macdonald and
Canada's Problem—Cape Colony, and our African Imperial
Interests—The Cape Premier—Australia and the Austral-
asian Group—Mr. Froude's Prophetic Denunciation, and
his Marvellous Insight—The Principal Difficulties in the
Way of Imperial Commercial Union discussed — The
Duties of an " Imperial Senate "—India, and the Crown
Colonies — The *Statist* Prize of 1,000 Guineas — The
Elements of Future Imperial Greatness and Prosperity
bound up in the Adoption of the Principles of the Com-
mercial Union of the Empire.

IN speaking or writing of the British Empire as it
presently exists, as a fact, it is to be remembered
always, at the same time, that it is in many respects
an incompleted fact. Its unity is yet only of the
most elementary character.

The British citizen, however, especially, and even
the colonial fellow-citizens, or fellow-subjects, have a
bond upon it for its more complete unity, arising in
the first place out of the sacrifices of blood, of treasure,
and endurance which its gradual acquisition has cost;
and, in the second place, from the necessity both of
the United Kingdom, or mother country, and its

colonies and scattered possessions themselves; of the continued supremacy over them *all;* of the same flag, and the protection derivable to the whole from the same symbol.

Fate, to whose unforeseen decision it was largely left at first, is now revealing, through lessons of experience and of hope, the necessities, the advantages, and the possibilities of an organic union, the ligaments of which have already been strung by the common language, the family ties, and the commercial intercourse common to them all.

It is mainly through commerce that the material satisfaction and compensation for the dependence and inter-dependence of the various parts with each other and the whole can be realised.

The diffusion of British capital, as well as of population throughout those vast areas on the credit of ample resources yet to be developed, has determined the greater importance of commercial union over every other bond.

The capital of the colonies being borrowed from the unconsumed labour results and property of Great Britain, and not the accretions of their own internal labour and exchanges, the necessity is laid upon the creditor and the debtors alike to perfect the organic system by means of which their necessary and mutual obligations to each other—for the past, the present, and the future—can alone be fulfilled.

Military and naval connection alone; financial connection alone; official and symbolic connection alone—even accompanied by diplomatic influence and control; telegraphic, postal, and shipping connection alone—will not create or maintain this necessary *solvent* union.

The resources on the credit of which the capitals were borrowed, and the necessities to both the United Kingdom and the colonies, arising out of their actual relations, cannot have development or satisfaction, unless PROFITABLE MARKETS AND EXCHANGES OVER THE AREA OF OBLIGATION AND DEPENDENCE ARE CREATED, ESTABLISHED AND SUSTAINED.

The hour has more than arrived when this has got to be done.

It is not an exhibition of pumpkins at the Imperial and Colonial Institute in London, nor yet of maps and charts of no man's land under the British flag hung up there, or anywhere else ; nor yet visits of royal princes to the antipodes ; it is not these that will ensure the *solvent union.*

The solvent union is a stern matter of business. Its practical consideration has been delayed too long, and it has been delayed in a vain and unpardonable ignorance of the *via media*, due to taking things for granted, which our adherence to the Free Trade formula precluded from possibility.

We vainly took for granted, for instance, that the development of Canada, with advantage to Canada and ourselves, was quite compatible with our abolishing all duties upon Norwegian timber and American wheat ; we vainly imagined, in such circumstances, that Canada would give us a monopoly of supplying her population with manufactures, whatever exclusive or fiscal imposts she should impose upon United States or other foreign competing products. We applied exactly the same absurd logic to our other colonies ; and that, after stimulating our emigration thither, and lending them millions of money !

The basis of the solvent union is a very simple one. It is founded, itself, upon the rock of justice, which, after all, is the true expediency for nations as well as for individuals.

It is simply that, by means of preferential terms, or preferences in respect to fiscal and protective duties, the disadvantages of geographical distance should be abolished, and the productions, for the most part, of the British colonies and of the United Kingdom should be made *economically nearer* to each other's markets than the similar productions of any foreign State.

In considering the practicability of this a little more closely, the following subjects claim our attention :—

I. The alternative of political disintegration and social revolution which threatens to overtake the British Empire.

II. The necessity that commercial union, if adopted, should be a binding as well as a voluntary arrangement, and that no single one, or several, of the contracting Parliaments should be at liberty thereafter suddenly to disturb or alter the Imperial commercial arrangements.

III. The necessity that a central Imperial control should be established, responsible to, and representative of, the estates at stake.

IV. That separate conditions, in harmony with the same policy, should be provided in respect to India and the Crown colonies, and that the basis of such should be, that it should be made so strongly their interest to fall in with the commercial union policy, that they would be drawn into it, apart from any direct representative and responsible position in the Imperial Council, it being politically impracticable to enfranchise subject races to equality with British subjects in the United Kingdom and the self-governing colonies.

V. The elements of future Imperial greatness and prosperity bound up in the adoption of the principles of the commercial union of the Empire.

In the first place :—

" The alternative of political disintegration and social evolution which threatens to overtake the British Empire."

The demand for Irish Home Rule,—Home Rule all round—and even Indian Home Rule—that demand is the first note of this alternative. Unless we proceed in constructive and comprehensive welding of our empire together, in bonds of mutual interest, our expansion, as it has gone on, will end in ruin and disintegration.

There is only one postulate upon which our adherence to Free Trade, and leaving our colonies to their fate, could be argued. It is, that the nations geographically nearer to us than our colonies are, should be converted to Free Trade, and converted very speedily. Of this there is not the remotest chance. Why should there be ? And, further, we cannot now afford to leave our colonies to their fate. We are like the principal creditor in analogous cases of a smaller character, who is compelled to save his estate by

absorbing or uniting his business with the business of
his debtor.

Sir John Macdonald (Canada's Grand Old Man), with
far-seeing statesmanship, as well as patriotism and
loyalty to the British connection, expressed Canada's
problem and the sentiment of millions of voices alike
in the utterances and public action which distinguished
his political career.

Mr. J. A. Froude, in a letter to the *Times*, October
10, 1888, says:—"It is as sure as the multiplication
table, that if we do not offer Canada such a union, the
Americans will, and the Canadian Dominion will be
practically lost to us. If there is any real hope for an
internal commercial union, I shall regard the work as
done, and it may not be too late to save Canada."

For the ordinary reader Canada's peculiar problem,
which has been here generally stated, may be further
amplified thus :—Canada with her industries and resources and obligations developed up to a certain
point, on account of her separate existence as a self-
governing colony, is denied her advantage of the
market of seventy millions of people across her
boundary line, while, at the same time, on account of
our commercial policy and Free Trade treaties, she is
denied other methods of extending her trade, and
especially the greatest and most certain of all—that
of either giving or receiving preferential terms in respect to the three hundred millions of British subjects
with whom she is in nominal relation under the British
flag. This constitutes for Canada the political and
economic question whose gravity has been so accur-
ately described by Mr. Froude in the quotation I

have just given.   Further, that this may not be
considered a mere party view of the situation, I have
only to refer the reader to the fact of the existence
and activity in Canada, by virtue of the reasons
stated, of an annexation to the U.S.A. party-policy,
headed by Professor Goldwin Smith, and the " Little
England " party.   I may further illustrate this aspect of the question, that is, the alternative of further
disintegration, by the case of Cape Colony.   At
the present moment the premier of that colony is
striving to avert in the interest of Cape Colony precisely the same impending dangers which Sir John
Macdonald did for Canada.

Cape Colony, the key-stone of our African Imperial
interests, is very much in the position of Canada.
She is surrounded by independent territories and
growing populations, and is hampered by the same
impediments to her expansion through her loyalty to
the British connection under the present state of
affairs.

The speech of the Cape premier, given *en extenso* in
the preceding chapter, pages 222-3, is a graphic and
ominous statement of this position.

Take the case of Australia and the Australasian
group of British possessions.   These have a not less
vital interest in a commercial union policy; and Great
Britain in relation to them is not less vitally interested in the necessity that the disadvantages of
geographical distance should be compensated by a
scheme of preference in respect to fiscal and protective duties.   Let us examine this a little closely.
These great and rising commonwealths will assuredly

break the bounds some day if the necessities of their
future development are not determined finally by the
attractions and advantages offered in an Imperial
commercial policy. What this will signify to Great
Britain is a subject of the most momentous import.
They, like Canada and Cape Colony, will have to
turn their attention, for the purposes of trade expansion, to those foreign territories and populations
with whom they also are in closer geographical relation than with Great Britain. The only alternative
before them, should preference over foreigners in
British and colonial markets be denied them, is to
set themselves to closer federation with each other
for fiscal and protective purposes, and to making the
best use of their position, geographically, on the
ocean routes to the Indian and Chinese seas, and to
the pacific sea-board. We must remember that not
only is the Australasian group in closer geographical
connection to these than to the mother country, but
also, that they are closer, geographically, to them
than the United Kingdom is. The Anglo-Saxon race
there will not allow the Germans to reap the advantage of our neglect of Imperial responsibility in this
respect, as they—the Germans—are busily endeavouring to do. Our Free Trade policy has environed us
in a fool's paradise. We must remember that there
is no possibility or probability, in the nature of things,
of the extension of Free Trade relations with the
European nations, or even with the United States of
America ; and the Australian nationalities will not,
and cannot, commit themselves, so far as the external
world is concerned, to a free import policy. They

may widen, as occasion offers, their area of free domestic exchanges, but this will be accompanied always (should commercial union with the empire be denied them) by protection against the outside world —including Great Britain—in spite of all our Free Trade policy and commercial treaties.

Twenty years ago, in the vain dream of a cosmopolitan Free Trade, the apostles of that policy coolly proclaimed to the world that they could view with equanimity the repudiation by the mother country of her colonial children ; to-day, under this disillusion, effected by successful foreign competition and successful foreign protection, the question has become that of those colonial children repudiating the mother country.

Mr. Froude, in his famous essays, following upon the steps of Carlyle and Ruskin, in prophetic denunciation of the moral iniquity of our political economy, has described most graphically the interest which Great Britain has in her progressive expansion of surplus capital and population, under a protective and Imperial direction of the same, in connection with her colonies. He discloses with marvellous insight the social disintegration which is already at work under *laissez-faire*, and sets in very clear language the inevitable prospect, should no wise departure from it be made, of the working classes of the United Kingdom, oppressed by its inhumanities, while at the same time enfranchised by political power, adopting wild measures for the relief of their class.

" They see," he writes, " their masters growing in

splendour and luxury. They see their own condition unimproved, and, under the existing system, unimprovable. They see the soil of England becoming the demesne of an ever-diminishing number of fortune's favourites, and their cherished idea, it is well known, is a re-division of the land, and their own restoration to a share in the general inheritance. They know that the land laws of England are different from the land laws of any other country in the world. They do not ask how far the monopoly which they deprecate may be due to causes which legislation did not produce and cannot remedy. They do not inquire what the effect would be of a violent disturbance of landed tenures, or how far they would obtain from a division of the soil the happiness they anticipate. They insist that the land is national property, and they demand that they shall be no longer excluded from their natural rights.

"Men possessed with an idea cannot be reasoned with. Divide England, Scotland, and Ireland as they will, two-thirds of our thirty millions could not live on the produce of the land, and an interference with the rights of property would paralyse manufactures, and destroy the means of support for the rest. As little can the Trade Unions do for the distribution of the profits of labour with their arbitrary restrictions upon work, and their wild notions of a dead level of reward, where the idle and incapable shall share alike with the skilful and industrious. The problem as they approach it is insoluble. They are like children grasping at the moon. Nevertheless, it is in these directions that their thoughts are running, and

sooner or later the organisation of the unions will be
turned upon politics, and upon securing a majority in
the House of Commons to carry out these notions.
The gin and beer are doubtless elements of Conservatism.   The satisfaction of the vulgar politician
at the increased consumption of such things is not
without reason.   The thriftless vagabond, who carries
his week's wages on Saturday afternoon to the pot-
house, and emerges out of his bestiality on Tuesday
morning to earn the materials for a fresh debauch—
this delightful being has nothing politically dangerous
about him.   He will sell his vote to the highest
bidder, and look no further than his quart of half-
and-half.   The working men, however, as a body,
are alive to the disgrace of their order.   Some day or
other they may check for themselves what they have
vainly petitioned the Legislature to assist them in
restraining, and whether or no, the present elements
of confusion in English society are sufficiently threat-
ening.   If we allow our industrial system to extend
in the same manner, and at the same rate of increase
as hitherto, every feature most fraught with danger
must increase along with it.   The boundary line between rich and poor will be more and more sharply
defined.   The number of those who can afford to
hold land must diminish as by a law of nature.   The
wealthy will become more wealthy, the luxurious
more luxurious, while there will be an ever-enlarging
multitude, deeply tinctured with mere heathenism,
left to shift for themselves, and resentful of the
neglect, with the cost of living keeping pace with the
advance of wages, and therefore in the presence of an

enormous accumulation of capital, condemned, apparently for ever, to the same hopeless condition, and yet with political power in their hands if they care to use it. No one who is not wilfully blind can suppose that such a state of things can continue. Human society is made possible only by the observance of certain moral conditions ; and tendencies which, if not positively immoral, are yet not positively moral, but material and mechanical, must and will issue at last in a convulsive effort to restore the social equilibrium."

In Chapter II., " Foolish Hopes and False Issues," allusion is made to these very aspects of our condition described by Mr. Froude. It is there pointed out that the popular unrest and suffering induced by the Free Trade policy is, for want of wiser alternatives, seeking more and more to remedy social miseries by organic changes. These changes, it must also be noticed, are notoriously of a destructive, and not of a constructive, character.

They assume entirely the character of civil war, of confiscation, and of plunder, and no arrestment of this tendency is at all possible under a policy of simply burying the faculties of observation and self-preservation in the desert sand in face of the impending storm.

The reader may also be referred to other observations on the same topic in Chapter XV., " The Fate of Being Undeceived—A Day of Reckoning."

In the second place, " The necessity that Commercial Union, if adopted, should be a binding as well as a voluntary arrangement, and that no single

one, or several, of the contracting Parliaments should
be at liberty thereafter suddenly to disturb or alter
the Imperial commercial arrangements." This consideration invests the subject with additional urgency,
because it recognises at once the principal difficulties
in the path of the adoption and the success of any
scheme of Imperial commercial union.   Its force
consists in the operation of democratic institutions,
both at home and in the great colonies.   It goes,
without saying, that any comprehensive arrangement,
which includes the United Kingdom and self-governing colonies in a scheme of reciprocal obligation, must
be voluntarily adopted by all the contracting parties.
It is not so fully recognised, however, that any such
arrangement or contract, once it is adopted, must be
binding—at least, for a considerable period—and not
liable to being made the sport of contending parties
and fluctuating majorities in the respective Parliaments.   The process which would be begun, under
such an arrangement, would be that of a new organisation and distribution of capitals, of population, and
of industrial enterprise.   Mercantile ramifications
founded upon these; new fleets of merchantmen;
new systems of docks and railroads, in addition to
those already existing; new corporations with or
without parliamentary charters; new Government
concessions for great undertakings; and even new
protectorates over subject and barbarous races, waiting
the advance of a strong beneficent civilisation, would
all ensue, and only in the permanency of the policy
which gave birth to these could the hopes connected
with their existence be realised.

The recent severe industrial troubles in the United
States of America, to a very large extent due to the
M'Kinley policy being disturbed (although also to a
larger extent due to the disturbance caused by the
silver question in that country), has shown what a
serious danger there is in first encouraging and
attracting investments of capital to new industrial
developments by a protective policy, and then allow-
ing confidence in these undertakings to be destroyed,
by making that policy the subject of party intrigue and
contention.   It is a warning to all who contemplate
the practical aspects of commercial union of the
British Empire of the imperative nature of the condition laid down under this head.

Now, to our third point :—

" That a central Imperial control shall be established, responsible to, and representative of, the
estates at stake."

An Imperial senate must be pre-supposed in connection with the political aspects of the question.
This senate would provide the central control referred to ; it would review and ratify the fiscal
arrangements of the separate self-governing colonies ;
it would assess and apportion the application of
Imperial revenue derived from the Imperial customs ;
it would organise the resources and industries of each
and every part, according to climatic and geographical advantages, in harmony with Imperial interests.

Among the resources which would require to be
organised and pursued is systematic State-aided
emigration.   No longer would Great Britain be
apathetic in the direction of her emigration, and the

emigrant, instead of settling in the United States of America, would settle in Canada, Australia, or the Cape ; and so our surplus population would be spread over British colonies, tending to the indefinite and magnificent expansion of the British Empire.

I now come to the fourth aspect of my subject, which I simply re-state :—

" That separate conditions, in harmony with the policy of Imperial commercial union, should be provided in respect to India and the Crown colonies, and that the basis of such should be, that it should be made so strongly their interest to fall in with the commercial union policy that they would be drawn into it, apart from any direct representative and responsible position in the Imperial Council, it being, politically, impracticable to enfranchise subject races to equality with British subjects in the United Kingdom and the self-governing colonies."

CONCLUSION.

THE fifth and last point:—

"The elements of future Imperial greatness and prosperity bound up in the adoption of the principles of the commercial union of the empire."

Mr. Cobden and his disciples were woefully self-deceived when they deprecated the expansion of the empire, and fondly imagined that Free Trade would open up vast markets all over the world for British goods. We are living in times when there can be no such illusions, for the theories of the Manchester School are shattered by the logic of events.

We can no longer dream of a " calico millennium," and the United Kingdom as the world's great workshop. The Commonwealth cannot rest upon our manufacturing supremacy, for it no longer exists; manufacturing England is stripped and bare, not only in the world's markets but in her home market.

The grave questions of the hour are, what to do to get trade and wages for our present congested populations, and what are we to do to secure our home and colonial markets and profitable exchanges? Meditation among the ruins and tombs of Free Trade will not supply an answer to these questions. We have drifted into a slough of misery and disappointment by following the Free Trade Will-o'-the-wisp policy. We have confusion in our industries, and social miseries springing from the *laissez-faire* policy. We have gone along the wrong road.

What will give us hope for the future? (Hope is the fount and spring, the very essence and origin of energy in life, be it that of the individual or the nation.) What will stir our national life-blood, and make Englishmen go easily and hopefully with lightly bounding feet? The answer is, do justice to British labour and safeguard the interests of the British Empire; secure by a wise fiscal policy the markets of that empire for the producers of the empire, by preferences accorded and enforced in their favour.

Who can measure the importance of holding the British Empire together? Not only are our material and moral interests at stake, but our future existence as a great nation depends upon *permanent union.*

It is for the people of the United Kingdom to say if their priceless inheritance is to be squandered, or if all parts of it are to be inseparable. The recent Inter-Colonial Conference at Ottawa furnished the strongest link—the bond of preferential trade—by which the empire can be consolidated. Wielded together in this way it can afford to be independent, for it produces all that it needs for its own requirements. The only chance of security is to make ourselves strong; the only hope of future prosperity is by Britons holding their own.

The proprietors of the *Statist* in offering the prize of 1,000 guineas for the best scheme of an Imperial Customs Union, remark :—

Q

"They have long considered the question of Imperial Federation as the really vital one before British statesmen. They believe that Imperial Federation will be only a word without a customs union between Great Britain and her colonies. . . . . . If this country is to hold in the future the great position among the nations which she now holds, for their welfare not less than for her own, it is essential that her people should have room to grow indefinitely. . . . . . And in our colonies we have that room, where the British people can multiply and replenish the earth. To bind together the colonies and the mother country with cords so strong as to defy the powers of breaking is, then, the most important task before British statesmanship. This is not a mere selfish English view ; it is really as much to the interest of the colonies as of ourselves that the British Empire should be maintained in ever-increasing strength. Putting aside pride of race, attachment to the old flag, the distinction conferred by citizenship in one of the very greatest empires the world has ever seen, it is surely of the most material advantage to every colonist, as well as to every resident in the United Kingdom, that the empire should be strong enough to impose respect upon the disturbers of the peace, and to insure protection if compelled to draw the sword. . . . . . Everyone admits the desirability of federation as a mere abstract proposition ; but too many shake their heads and dismiss it as a utopia impossible of realisation. We are sorry to say that those who pooh-pooh are more numerous and more influential here at home than in the colonies ; and perhaps it is not surprising that

that should be so. The real difficulty in the way of federation is the different tariff policies of the mother country and some of the colonies. All other questions could be arranged if there was goodwill upon both sides. But the tariff difficulty is a very real one, and we are willing to admit that it will tax our statesmanship to remove it in a satisfactory way. It is because we feel this so strongly that we invite the co-operation of all who are interested in the greatness and the permanence of the empire in devising some scheme which will work and stand criticism for bringing about a customs union between the United Kingdom and the colonies."

Mr. Gladstone takes up the old position that any proposal which attacks Free Trade is unworthy of consideration, for he has written in the *Statist*:— " The authority of the *Statist* is great, and the prize is magnificent, but I do not feel myself qualified to take any part in the proceedings now contemplated until (1) I can see a better prospect of obtaining a practical result, and (2) am satisfied that a mode has been found of forming such a union without its involving any secession to the principle of Protection."

Mr. Gladstone is still wedded to Free Trade, but will the people of Great Britain persist in their present fiscal system ? If so, they will fail to reap the advantages which a *true* Imperial and commercial union would readily afford them. There is no escape, therefore, if we would secure the benefits of Imperial Commercial Federation of the British Empire and the mighty possible future of Great Britain, from a return to wise, necessary and scientific protection of our Imperial Commonwealth.

To persevere in a disintegrating policy, in spite of the plainest warnings, is inexpressible folly.

If British statesmen understood their business, they would gather Britain's colonies close to her ; but, alas ! they feed the electorate of the United Kingdom with party catch-words, cant, and fine phrases, and delusive promises. The ocean empire of Great Britain—where millions of her sons can spread over their broad inheritance—is not thought of in the party wrangling, babblement, and scramble for political power. Such is the deplorable condition into which the executive administration of the British Empire seems to have fallen.

The reader's attention is directed to the following extract from " Oceana," page 338 (all honour to the patriotic man who placed his statesman-like views before his fellow-countrymen) :—

" If the colonies are to remain integral parts of Oceana, it will be through the will of the people. To the question, What value are they? the answer is, that they enable the British people to increase and multiply. The value of the British man lies in his being what he is—another organic unit, out of the aggregate of which the British nation is made ; and the British nation is something more than a gathering of producers and consumers and tax-payers : it is a factor, and one of the most powerful, in the development of the whole human race. By its intellect, by its character, by its laws and literature, by its sword

and cannon, it has impressed its stamp upon mankind with a print as marked as the Roman. The
nation is but the individuals who compose it, and the
wider the area over which these individuals are growing, the more there will be of them, the stronger they
will be in mind and body, and the deeper the roots
which they will strike among the foundation-stones of
things. These islands are small, and are full to over-
flowing. In the colonies only we can safely multiply,
and the people, I think, are awakening to know it.
It may be otherwise. It may be that the people
will say that the days of empires are past, that we
are all free now, we are our own masters and must
look out for ourselves each in our own way. If this
be their voice, there is no remedy. As they decide,
so will be the issue. But it was not the voice of
America. It need not be the voice of scattered
Britain ; and if we and the colonies alike determine
that we wish to be one, the problem is solved. The
wish will be its own realisation. Two pieces of cold
iron cannot be welded by the most ingenious ham-
mering ; at white heat they will combine of themselves. Let the colonists say that they desire to be
permanently united with us ; let the people at home
repudiate as emphatically a desire for separation, and
the supposed difficulties will be like the imaginary
lion in the path—formidable only to the fool or the
sluggard. No great policy was ever carried through
which did not once seem impossible. Of all truly
great political achievements the organisation of a
united empire would probably be found the easiest."

In conclusion, I consider, briefly, the elements of
hope involved in the policy of commercial union of
the empire.

Under this head a variety of considerations arise,
which are of peculiar interest to the United Kingdom
in the first place, and secondly, but of no less importance, to the detached portions of the empire.

To the United Kingdom two very important considerations may be noted. The first consists in the
ample and favourable opportunities which such a
scheme will provide for supplies of raw material,
surplus food, bullion, etc., for our industrial and trade
requirements. Thirty years ago, when Free Trade
ideas had some plausibility, it was the fashion to consider our British population to be dependent upon
China for tea, which was fast becoming a necessity of
life; to be dependent upon the United States of
America for cotton; upon Russia and the Baltic ports
for grain, hides, flax, etc., in addition to similar imports from other foreign States, and it was loudly
declared that as all such necessary purchases from
foreigners would necessitate equal purchases on their
part of British manufactures, our paramount interest
lay in cultivating this cosmopolitan exchange.

The colonies, and a colonial policy, therefore, were
judged to be of an exceedingly secondary and
subordinate importance. We have lived to see the
fallacy of these declarations and beliefs. We have
lived to see our markets taken advantage of by
foreign States to the detriment of our colonies, and
the successful development under high Protection on
the part of these States (upon whom we made our-

selves so unnecessarily dependent) of their industrial capacity in competition with our claim to be the workshop of the world.

The foreigner, whom we have so favoured at the expense of our own citizens, has taken from us in return only what has exactly suited his own national interest, and has used every advantage and facility afforded by geographical position, and our folly, with complete indifference to British interests, of any kind in question.

The foreigner has bought coal, wool, machinery, and every crude product or important tool which would enable him, while enjoying our free market for his surplusses, to do without our finished labour products. Under our precipitate adoption of free imports from all quarters, the foreigner was under no necessity of doing otherwise.

But, during the past thirty years, the growth of our empire abroad, the expansion of our productive area in India, Canada, Australasia, and the Cape —along with improved facilities of transit—has presented Great Britain with the magnificent prospect of equal independence of the foreigner ; provided—and only with this *proviso*—that Great Britain resumes her Imperial and preferential relation to these great colonies and dependencies.

The old position and argument of the cosmopolitan Free Trader is abolished and swept away by the practical ability and capacity of our own productive areas abroad to supply us with every necessity, under a Protective system, our demand for which was the pretext for our hasty adoption of free imports.

India can send us the productions of all lands and all climates—cotton, silk, jute, rice, spices, tea, etc. Canada can supply abundant wheat, timber, furs, and hundreds of other useful products. The West India Islands, with a tropical climate, are adapted by nature to supply us with many productions.

Australasia and the Cape offer us unlimited advantages of a suitable nature, and all of these are prepared, in return for an effective preference in our markets, to extend an equally effective preference to our manufactures over those of foreign States.

But there is more in all this than appears upon the surface. The study of scientific Protection assures any one who devotes sufficient thought to existing economic conditions abroad, that foreign States which have been partially exploited under our Free Trade policy are, and would still be, under a policy of wise Protection and Imperial preference on our part, dependent upon the British market for the consumption of their vast surplusses. Great Britain would still be their necessary and their best market for all surplusses over their own powers of consumption. What then? Then would come in *the real bargaining power of a Protective policy.*

The colonies and India would be assured of our market by preferential terms. The competing productions of foreign States would still have to seek our markets, but *subject to the fiscal burdens which equity demanded that they should have imposed upon them by this and other British Governments for the advantage of the British Empire.*

Suppose, for instance, that we should admit Indian

tea at a preference of 15 per cent. over that of China, what would the result be in the matter of our trade relations with China? China, being practically more dependent upon our market for the consumption of her tea harvests, than Great Britain is upon China for the consumption of surplus cotton or other manufactures, would have to sell her tea at a reduction of 15 per cent. in price to share the market in competition with India. Precisely similar results, to a greater or less degree, would follow with every other foreign product depending upon our vast market, in competition with the *preferentially treated products of the British Empire.*

The hour has arrived when a tax can be imposed with advantage upon the wealth and productions which our trade has fostered abroad, to the economic advantage, be it repeated, both of the United Kingdom and her colonies and possessions over the world.

But the incidence of such an impost would most probably induce offers from the States most hardly hit, to purchase some remission, by extending favours to British exported manufactures imported by them, greater and more exclusive than any commercial treaties under so-called Free Trade have been able to secure.

We have no retaliation to fear from nations dependent upon our markets, and under the necessity of submitting to our wisely-directed fiscal regulations. We have great concessions and advantages to expect, and to confidently predict, as the outcome of such an Imperial and provident policy.

There is another consideration, the value of which

can hardly be overestimated, in looking ahead to the industrial future of Great Britain. It is this, that under a scheme of commercial union—and the political union, in any case—of a general character, which such a policy would necessitate, Great Britain could look calmly forward to maintaining her *central* position in regard to the world's trade. It is this central position which is otherwise certain to be lost under the adjustments of capital and labour in the competition which is going on, and in the present unsatisfactory state of our relations with our colonies and dependencies in the matter of trade. The central position would be lost whenever the seat of manufactures, in which we were formerly supreme, gets shifted or divided through the separate and inorganic competition of British capital in different quarters of the globe.

The original idea of colonies was that of plantations, and not by any means that to which we have been drifting, of establishing separate commonwealths, to be eventually left to their fate, and to make the most of their position and resources without reference to each other or to the mother country.

Following up this original idea, the development of industries in our various colonies would be capable of systematic direction and expansion in harmonious union with, and subordination to, the interests of the whole. As matters presently exist, there is a menace to the industrial population of the United Kingdom in many of the enterprises and developments sustained by British capital in India, and even in our colonies. The establishment of cotton mills and of factories for other finished products on the Indian seaboard, for instance, under the leave-alone system is calculated to imperil our hold for the United Kingdom upon the Eastern markets, and to degrade British labour by the direct competitive conflict of barbarism and semi-barbarism with it in industrial competition.

It would be much more natural for the labouring population of India to be growing crude products in the fields for British labour to manufacture, or British luxury to consume, than to have India and other British territories under the exigencies of competition, becoming rivals and competitors for possession of the same kind of business.

What we have, as a possible future under an Imperial commercial policy, is, not the planting of manufacturing populations along the seaboard of our most favoured territories, but the diffusion of population over extended areas of production, with railway, river, and canal means of communication from the centre to the seaboard and from province to province. This manner of development would promote an organisation of industry throughout the empire of co-ordinate and reciprocal advantage, and entirely fulfilling the great mission of organic expansion of our empire, with the fullest advantage to the United Kingdom, as the mother country, and to the lasting advantage of the colonies and other British possessions themselves.

THE END.